Praise for Yc

"Elizabeth Cabalka has created a process so needed in these distracted and fractured times. These words offer wholeness and healing and a sense of a companion for the ups and downs of life's journey."

> — *Sally Howell Johnson, author of*
> *The Practicing Life: Simple Acts, Sacred Living and*
> *Barefoot Zone: Walking the Sacred Path*

"Who among us has not felt a sense of deep longing? Longing so deep, so intense, and so unknown that it can stop us in our tracks? Longing for expression, for an authentic work and personal life, for connection to the Divine already within us? Elizabeth Cabalka with *Yoga Expression Spirit - Tools for Authentic Living* gives us a new kind of toolkit, simple, refined, effective. Part memoir and reading like a novel, her book illuminates the way to discover your deep longing."

> — *Marcia Appel, Green Lotus founder and*
> *teacher, author, and former corporate executive*

"This book is an incredible reminder of how important it is to show up for your life, to let your inner child out to create and play, to take time to slow down and smell the roses! Elizabeth shares yogic philosophies in an accessible way that creates opportunities for the reader to wake up and live today."

> — *Tory Schaefer, National Presenter and*
> *Director of LifePower Yoga*

Yoga Expression Spirit –

Tools for Authentic Living

By Elizabeth Cabalka

Portions of this book were originally published in the
online blog: yogaexpressionspirit.wordpress.com

Library of Congress Control Number: 2016917030

Cabalka, Elizabeth, 1964-
Yoga Expression Spirit – Tools for Authentic Living
ISBN 978-0-9744062-3-7

Artwork and Cover Design by John Gerber

Author Photo by Amanda Dambowy

Published in the United States by Fuzion Print

For my mother,
who never ceases to inspire me.
I love you, Mom.

Table of Contents

AN INVITATION   1

YES   5

YES – The Pieces   11

Why YES?   19

The Cost   25

Mind-Body Relationship   31

YOGA

Y is for Yoga   39

Collaboration Begins as an Inside Job   43

Listening Deeply. Responding Kindly.   49

Healing the Inner Divide   57

EXPRESSION

The Puzzle   67

Inside Out   71

The Power of Uncomfortable   77

LOL   85

Busy   91

Life Making   97

SPIRIT

Mystery   **105**

Inhale. Exhale. Repeat.   **107**

The Veil   **113**

Eighty-Eight Hawks   **119**

Seeds **129**

The Unexpected   **133**

AUTHENTIC LIVING

Coming Home   **139**

Where Do You Live?   **143**

What Brings You Alive?   **149**

Revere the Rake?   **155**

Say YES   **157**

Acknowledgements   **159**

Artwork   **161**

About the Author **162**

An Invitation

Hello, friend. I am so glad we found each other.

I do not know what brought us together, but I am grateful for the opportunity to share some thoughts about authentic living and three tools that make this possible. May this book land softly with you.

When I was hurting, deeply sad, broken, and brittle, I wrote this book to return to myself and to heal. This book was borne from a deep longing to live my authentic life, kindly, simply, bravely, and openly. Living authentically meant aligning my talents with my days. It meant living in a way that did not require me to negotiate with my integrity, in a way that aligned my words and actions with my True-North, to win without requiring others to lose, and collaborating with others toward a meaningful end.

Equal to my longing was a fear that authentic living was out of reach or that I was not worthy of such a thing. You see, the seeds of my authentic self were sown in a small pot, just about the size of my sense of self-worth. All my inner voices and past programming had placed that pot in a dark corner of my heart. Too little sunshine. Too little water. The sprouting seeds were dying. And so was I. This book is the result of reaching, with hope, toward a small bit of light barely illuminating a promise-filled path.

I arrived at a moment in which I could no longer move through each day as a slave to my out-of-control and often unkind thoughts. I no longer fit the mold of the life I thought I was supposed to be living. One day I knew it was time. This was it – a do-or-die moment. I wanted more. With no small amount of bravery, I stepped into all that was possible and waiting – seeds already sprouted within me.

Through the writing of this book I returned to myself and created a new life. This is my hope for you. This is not an exhaustive, clinical, how-to book. Rather, it is a nudge of encouragement to be kind to yourself, to return to your body, to engage in this moment, and to dance daily with mystery.

Do you feel disconnected from the authentic you or far away from who you want to become? Do you sense something calling to you but your inner world is too loud to hear it? Is there something seeking expression through you but you are afraid to give it voice or energy, too concerned what others may think or say? Are you simply out of sorts and don't know where to turn? I offer you these gifts – **Y**oga **E**xpression **S**pirit – as tools for reconnection, for creation, and for expression of your authentic life.

If a deep longing is calling to you, the seed is already planted. That *something* already **is** and has life. It simply needs your attention. How much longer can you ignore it?

I invite you to say Y E S to your authentic life.

Elizabeth Cabalka

4

YES

"If something doesn't change, I am going to have a heart attack."

The third time I repeated those words, alarm bells sounded. I couldn't allow myself to repeat this insight without corrective action. I needed to do something NOW.

I was fifty-one years old and I was deeply sad. Each day I was aware that I was not living the life I wanted to live. As I repeated the dire prediction, I felt the nudge of something deep inside me that was seeking expression. There was important work to do, songs to sing, music to play, books to read, a book to write, and a beautiful world to explore. All of this was covered, however, by the daily grind. The light was buried and everything seemed dark.

The longing I felt for a different life was not simply benign wishing. The vision and ideas that called to me felt so big. Enormous really and, at times, utterly overwhelming. They needed me. And I needed them. But the risks, oh the risks! Claiming a different future required bravery, releasing any sense of being a victim to circumstance, actively claiming my longing, no longer believing what I offered lacked value, stepping off an unpalatable but familiar pathway, and firmly taking the reins of my life. Possibly failing.

I vacillated between the deepest longing for a new life and a paralysis that it might actually manifest and I would have to change. Each cell told me this longing was not simply empty hope or a folly, but as necessary as oxygen. I had no idea whether new life was possible, yet I knew I was dying a little each day with the unexpressed gifts buried deep within me. I knew I needed to return to myself but had forgotten the way.

My dear husband looked on helplessly as I barricaded myself in the bedroom with the shades drawn on a glorious Sunday afternoon. Pencil in hand, I stared at a blank page in my journal. Where had I gone? Where was the joyful, creative, capable and authentic Elizabeth?

"What brings me back to myself?" I wondered aloud as I doodled in my journal.

Yoga.

That word captured the tool I had used time and again to return to myself. How often had I rolled out my mat, feeling fractured and brittle, only to rise from it sometime later restored and refreshed? Too many times to count or to ignore.

"What else brings me joy?" I thought. "Well, there is music and writing, painting and singing.... Hmmm."

Expression.

Yes, expression. The act of allowing creativity to flow freely with little regard for the outcome. Just flowing, simply allowing, without judgement. Expression was the key to uncapping my effervescence.

"What else? I know there is more. What keeps me in balance?"

Spirit.

Ah, Spirit. That presence within me that seeks meaning and is drawn to hope. The animating force of breathing deeply, acknowledging the unknown, and dancing daily with mystery, living mindfully, daily meditation…. Tending my Spirit.

I closed my eyes for a moment and took a deep breath, and then another. As I opened my eyes, I looked at the words on the page:

Yoga.

Expression.

Spirit.

Y E S!

I felt a surge of energy that had long been a stranger. This was my answer! These were the tools that brought me back to myself over and over. These were my tools for authentic living.

In the hour that followed, I outlined a book I knew I would write, retreats designed around these tools, as well as classes and coaching. I stepped into the refreshing, freely flowing river of my True Self. The seeds of expression within me, sown so long ago, were reaching for the light.

That day changed the course of my life. This book is an opportunity to share with you all that has transpired since that day. The gifts of returning to myself, of freely expressing something that can no longer be contained, of sharing these tools with others and watching them unearth their authentic selves, have allowed me to live on purpose and with purpose. I have returned to myself and to joyful living. This is my hope for you.

Come with me, friend. Authentic living awaits.

Elizabeth Cabalka

YES – The Pieces

"Just who on earth do you think you are, little miss-know-it-all?!" barked my harsh, deeply unkind, inner critic.

"**Y**oga **E**xpression **S**pirit, my foot! What are you *thinking*, taking on not just one but *three* broad and grand topics?! Don't you know you can fill a library (or two or three or more) with all the books and wisdom on any *one* of these mammoth subjects? What on *earth* do *you* think you can possibly add?"

There it was, my greatest fear, loud and proud, standing front and center. Boy, did that one get me all kinds of wrapped around the axle. I muddled through and wrestled with that one for a few days, nearly paralyzed with self-doubt. Who *did* I think I was? What *could* I possibly add? Perhaps I *was* a wee bit too big for my britches. These thoughts had their way with me, circular and judging, and I could feel myself shrinking with each passing day.

Just a few days earlier I had uncovered an answer that propelled me out of misery and into a new adventure. All the quiet certainty that arrived with that insight had almost entirely evaporated.

And then an even quieter, but equally powerful, inner voice interjected, "Dear one, listen. Who are you *not* to add your voice to the chorus?"

Of the many doubts, fears, and voices that daily dance through my head, this is the voice to which I diligently listen most closely. This is the thought that propels me forward.

It is true that some of the greatest wisdom thinkers and teachers have weighed in on these topics for millennia. There is nothing revolutionary that I can bring to these individual topics. Then again, I believe there is something of value in this message of their combined value to our authentic lives. That certainly is my hope.

All I can know for sure it that **Y**oga, **E**xpression and **S**pirit are the tools I use to return to my authentic self and to my authentic life. While I will not attempt to fully and universally define any one of these items, I can certainly share my understanding and experience of each separately and also collectively. It is with that intention that I offer these thoughts to you.

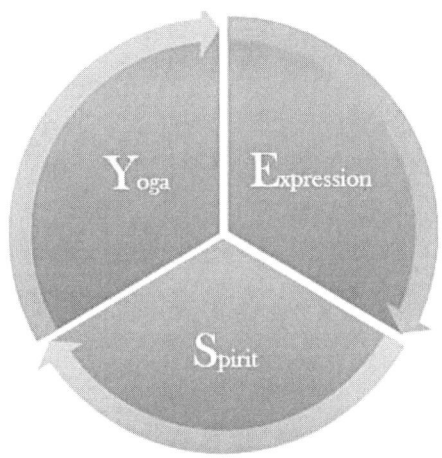

Y E S

Consider a wheel. It rolls most efficiently when it is 1) made of quality materials, 2) properly inflated, and 3) precisely balanced. Neglect any one of these factors and you will *kathunk* down the road. And so it is also with what I call the YES Wheel of our lives.

While I have visually represented these three tools as distinct and separate, in reality there are no lines to divide them. Each tool blends into the other, seamlessly connected. Just as there is but one wheel, the three factors for efficiency and effectiveness (and just plain 'roll-ability') are intertwined. When all three are functioning, the ride is smooth and enjoyable and the wheel is a non-issue. When even one factor is missing, forward motion can be impeded or even stopped.

For me, **Y**oga, **E**xpression, and **S**pirit are the Athos, Porthos, and Aramis of my authentic life. They defend, protect, feed, nourish, and support me. All for one and one for all.

For the purpose of clarity, I will briefly define each tool as I understand it to erect the framework.

'Y' is for Yoga

While the definition of yoga may differ widely based on the school of thought or discipline, the following definition serves me well:

Yoga – A science for living well, bringing mind, body, and breath together in the present moment.

14

While some think only of tight or scant clothing, lithe bodies, a guru-like teacher, and impossible-looking postures, these are a few of the many gifts that yoga provides me:

- A spring cleaning for the body and a good sweeping of the mental cobwebs
- Suppleness in the muscles for agility and flexibility
- Quiet in the body
- Quiet in the mind
- Spaciousness physically and mentally
- Preparation for meditation and creation.

'E' is for Expression

Expression – The process of bringing to life one's thoughts, insights, inspirations, or feelings.

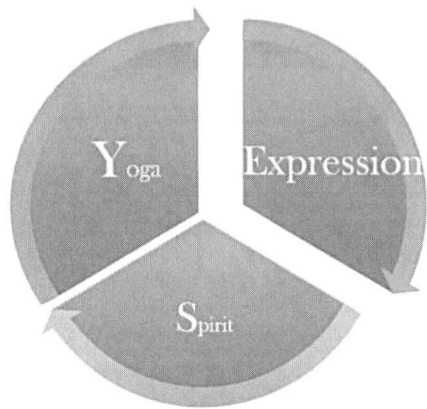

At its heart, expression is making or creating, drawing out, bringing forth and bringing to life. The gifts of expression that I readily experience are:

· A sense of being in the flow of life
· Inspiration
· Joy
· Creativity
· Authenticity
· Freedom
· Release
· A form of meditation.

In the throes of creative, authentic expression, my mind becomes quiet, focused, and calm. I am filled with the joy of making or creating.

'S' is for Spirit.

This is perhaps the most broad, deep, and sticky piece of the pie. In one respect, Spirit is an utterly unknowable Mystery. At the same time, Spirit is as close as our breath, the animating force. This is where my sensibilities lie.

Spirit – The Mystery we engage with and through our breath.

Through breath work, stillness, and meditation, I have come to know Spirit as:

17

- Mystery
- Life Force
- Inner Stillness
- Peace
- One-ness
- Inspiration.

Yoga **E**xpression **S**pirit – Y E S. By incorporating these three tools into your daily life, you can quiet your mind, live and love well, and create a spaciousness for the expression of your authentic life.

Why YES?

Calm. Focus. Attention. Listening. Self-awareness.

I am concerned that these skills are falling away in the world just when they are needed most desperately. The question that naturally follows is where do we learn the vanishing art of simply being present?

Let's first look at the realities of the world in which we live.

It is nearly a radical act of civil disobedience these days to power down and unplug. Distraction is rampant. Digital overload is epidemic. How odd that all this connection causes so much disconnection. People are disconnected from their body, from their breath, and from their own unique creative energy. It is the rare person who puts conscious boundaries around distraction, who makes sustained eye contact and limits information input to only the most critical. It is the rarest of individuals who can be fully present to another human, really listening not simply waiting to speak. And can we please just have a conversation without repeatedly pausing to go to the internet for some factoid we simply MUST KNOW NOW?!

In today's world, few seem to understand the role of technology. Like money, technology is a marvelous servant but a horrible master. As a result, we are a wildly distracted people, receiving enormous amounts of non-critical information each moment of the day, and focused on nothing of inherent inner value.

To be clear, I am not a Luddite, nor am I anti-technology. In fact, I spent much of my career working in the Information and Data Technology field and the irony is not lost on me that this book will be promoted via five forms of social media. I believe, however, that the collective and nearly exclusive attention given to technology and external tools has been over-emphasized at the cost of our most valuable *inner* resources.

I take our collective level of distraction very personally. I am an avid biker, both road riding and mountain biking. Of late, there has been an alarming increase in the number of biking fatalities at the hands of distracted drivers. Yes, I take this personally and spend my time on two wheels looking ahead closely and in my rear view mirror for the eyeballs of approaching drivers. If I see eyeballs, great. If not, I head for the ditch.

A friend shared with me recently her frustration with her boss. Every time she spoke up in a meeting, he used that moment to check his email on his phone, a passive aggressive way of demeaning her value. How many times have you seen a child tugging on a phone-gazing parent trying to get their attention? The truth is you cannot successfully fake attention. In fact, your undivided attention is a powerful tool and often can be the most valuable gift you can give someone.

In a world where there is no question for which we cannot find an immediate answer, we have forgotten that our answers rarely yell to be heard. Unless we are quiet inside, unless we are discerning about how much non-critical information we feed ourselves, we can miss important answers or nudges toward the path of our authentic life.

What about calm, focus, attention, listening and self-awareness?

In a yelling world, these skills are too often perceived as soft, valueless, passive, or easy. I beg to differ. These skills are deep and wide and burly and robust, requiring rugged discipline, commitment, and clarity about their incredible value to self and to the world. Sadly, they are not readily taught and they most certainly are not publicly modeled.

How and where, then, do we acquire and develop these skills?

Most people believe these skills are mental, originating strictly between the ears. That belief comes from a misunderstanding of the mind, which science shows resides not only in the brain but also in every cell of our body. Unless we calm the body, we can never fully calm the mind. And a calm mind is the foundation on which focus, attention, listening, and self-awareness reside.

This is my passion. **Yoga Expression Spirit** is my response to a world that wants to sell us our answers every moment of the day, a world heavily invested in making us believe we desperately need something external, complex, and costly to make ourselves whole. **Y**oga **E**xpression **S**pirit is about cultivating the skills to care for your body, calm your mind, allow the seeds of expression to grow, and reclaim your authentic life.

Are you ready? If so, here are a few questions to consider:

How much time each day do you spend on your attire? On your appearance? On your phone? Engaged in the external tools of your trade? What would happen if you made a little more time for your best resource – you?

The Cost

When the turbulence of our mental busyness subsides and our mind becomes still, a deep happiness naturally arises within. *– Geshe Kelsang Gyatso, Introduction to Buddhism*

The evening was perfect. I put on my hiking shoes and the dog danced eagerly as I fastened her collar. We headed out for our evening walk to enjoy what promised to be a glorious sunset. It was seventy-eight degrees and the breeze was warm and gentle. The only sounds were the evening settling chatter of the birds and the crunch of my shoes on the trail. Our closest neighbor was over one mile away. What a heavenly evening in the Sonoran desert.

The first impulse to grab my phone arrived precisely two minutes into our walk. I paused with my hand on my back pocket.

"No need to capture. Just enjoy," my inner wisdom whispered. We walked on.

Shortly I found myself reaching for my phone again as I remembered I had neglected to return a friend's call a few hours earlier.

"Nope, it can wait," I assured myself and wrestled my hand away from my back pocket.

We climbed the last few steps to the crest of a small mesa that afforded a spectacular 360 degree view of three mountain ranges, the setting sun, and the 21,000 acre park we called home in the winter for several years. I sat down on a rock and took in the vista, breathing deeply and slowly in an effort to calm my heart rate after the climb. The evening light brushed the mountains with a changing palette — first coral, then pink, then purple, then blue. What a gift, this moment, this view, this life!

And there went my hand again, reaching for my phone, this time to text two friends with whom I studied meditation, certain that it was imperative to share this moment with them. Right then. Had to!

"No, no, no! This is madness," I gently chastised. I took a breath and with a slow exhalation whispered, "Be here now, Elizabeth. Be. Here. Now."

I was suddenly acutely aware that this moment was a gift. Its value would not be determined by the number of Facebook 'Likes' or the fact that I shared a photo of it with a friend across the country. This moment needed no outside validation. Nor did I, despite my habitual need to somehow capture it all and offer it up for public consumption.

I took a breath, feeling the breath fill my lungs, the wave reaching for the heart and cresting there. The wave slowly receded and washed in again. With each breath I came back to myself and settled further into the moment.

The minutes that followed will not soon be forgotten, both supremely simple and exquisitely textured.

Breath. Light. Body. Color. Breeze. Mountains. Quiet. Creatures. Expansive. Contentedness. Beauty. Connectedness. Joy.

I waded deeply into my experience, feeling gently woven into it with each breath. A far different experience than simply waiting for the best photo angle and plotting a caption.

The Cost.

In the Meditation and Mindfulness class I teach, we dig deeply into the value of being mindfully present to life and the tools that support mindful living. We also talk about the cost of *not* being present to our lives. We talk at length about the ways in which we pay a hefty toll for our persistent busyness, multi-tasking and distractedness. The list of the ways we incur these costs is long but here are just a few items to consider:

Personal Safety and Physical Well-Being.

The price of distractedness to our personal safety and well-being is no laughing matter. Have you ever tripped or sustained injury (or, heaven forbid, injured someone else) because you were not paying attention or your mind was elsewhere?

Mentally.

Distraction, ruminating on the past or anticipating the what-if of the future all create anxiety, stress, even depression and cognitive diminishment.

Relationships.

The loneliest place in the world can be just a few feet away from the one you love when their phone or tablet is immensely more important than what you just said.

Your Authentic Life.

When we are not present to life, it passes us by, a gift unopened.

Next time you reach for the mobile device to capture or share, pause for a moment. Consider your motivation. Will the moment still matter if you do not try to capture it, if you do not publicly share it? Take a deep breath. Take another. Look around. Gaze deeply. Breathe. Ponder. Be still. Be present to your authentic life, the joys and the difficulties. Be in this moment and receive the gifts inherent in the Now.

Please do not misunderstand me. There is nothing wrong with sharing. At the same time, do not let your sharing become a two-dimensional substitute for a full experience of your authentic life, the wonder, the joy, the beauty and the mystery within and around you. I will work on this too.

Elizabeth Cabalka

Five Steps to a Healthy Mind-Body Relationship

As we reach for an authentic life, there is a pressing need to reconnect with the body and align our mental activities with our physical being. As an anecdote to the wildly destructive 'gerbil-on-a-wheel' mental chatter, yoga breathing and postures, called asanas, can be powerful and readily accessible tools for quieting both body and mind, bringing them together in this moment for a collaborative relationship.

But what if yoga is not your thing? That's just fine. Here are a few steps to start your journey inward.

Step One – Awareness of Your Thoughts. Everything begins with awareness. We cannot change that which we do not see. And, ironically, in this case we begin by closing our eyes for greater seeing. Sit quietly for a few moments. Initially, even one minute will suffice. Bring your awareness to your thoughts. Notice, without judgement, the patterns of your mind. Watch it run rapidly here and there. Listen to the tone of the dialog. Be kind to yourself. Just notice. Jot down what you hear. Do you notice repetitive or circular thinking? That's alright. This exercise is about bringing awareness to your thoughts, not judging these thoughts. Or, perhaps more aptly, bringing awareness to your judgement of your thoughts. Pause and listen as often as you can. Start with five deep breaths and turn your awareness inward. The practice of noticing deepens the skill of awareness. With awareness, you can choose differently.

Step Two – Tune Into Your Body. As you sit quietly and comfortably, breathing deeply and slowly, draw your awareness inward. Slowly scan your body, from the top of your head to the tip of your toes. Scan slooooooowly, pausing often. Notice sensations in your body and any thoughts that accompany these sensations. Take your time to become keenly aware of a limb or set of muscles. Listen as your attention moves from the corners of your eyes to the tip of your toes. Notice. What is your body saying? How do the many parts move together? Is there fluidity or brittleness? What have you decided about your body and its state of affairs? Be kind. Just notice. Perhaps capture your insights with the tip of a pencil on paper.

Step Three – Consider a New Thought That Draws You Toward a Kinder Response. When you come across an area of your body that triggers a strong thought or response, verbally repeat aloud what your mind is thinking. Mirror the tone and volume of the inner voice. Say it again and notice how it makes you feel. Are your words kind? Likely not. How long have you carried and repeated this thought? You may be very familiar with your inner voice or this may be the first time you have heard your inner dialog spoken aloud.

Now consider how you might think about a certain body part or muscle group differently. For example:

"I feel so stiff and uncomfortable! I am *such* a slug!" can become, "I notice it is time to gently move and stretch my body."

"Ugh, I hate my fat belly!" can become, "I am aware that my tummy reflects my eating habits and stress levels. Perhaps it is time to look at that and do something different."

You may not immediately sing a love song to your body, but try for something more neutral to soften the exchange. Notice how this new thought pattern feels. Is there less judgement? Perhaps place a note on the mirror with a newly fashioned phrase and say it aloud – kindly – next time you look at your reflection.

Step Four – Take Action Kindly Then Take Action Again. The most lasting change begins gently and consistently. Consider the powerful force of a glacier or the carving actions of a river. New thoughts and behaviors can feel foreign and uncomfortable. Since the body and mind default to familiar patterns that are deep and strong, know that you will be uncomfortable in your new behaviors for a while. Until you are not.

Let your changes be gentle. Perhaps today simply stand up from your desk periodically, stretching, breathing, and noticing for just one minute. Or how about taking three minutes somewhere in your day to breathe deeply and notice your body? Remember that you are learning a new language. Be patient. Study the messages and listen as you would to a new friend. Eagerly. Respectfully. Asking curious questions.

Step Five – Develop Your Yoga Practice. Yes, we are back to yoga. I believe yoga can be accessible to everyone, from children to octogenarians and beyond. It is a rich and deep tradition that is best experienced to fully know. After ten years, these are the gifts that my very basic but faithful yoga practice provides me each day:

- A spring cleaning for the body and a good sweeping of the mental cobwebs.
- A tool for suppleness in my muscles, for agility, posture, and flexibility.
- A quiet, calm, and vibrant body.
- A still, focused, and peaceful mind.
- A moving meditation and a preparation tool for seated meditation or creation.

Sound enticing? Developing your yoga practice can take many shapes such as finding a local class, DVD or teacher that fits your objectives and abilities. Or it may mean simply dusting off your yoga mat and recommitting to your practice. Whatever form it takes, be kind to your body as you begin, gently moving and breathing.

There on your yoga mat, or doing gentle stretches while seated in a chair, let your outer world fall away and allow your inner world come into focus. Become aware of your thoughts and the language of your body. Breathe deeply and draw yourself into the present moment, into your breath. Stay here a while. Be patient. Be persistent. Notice as the voices eventually fade and a gentle quiet seeps in. The pathway between mind and body is cleared and your greatest resources align in collaboration, right here and now.

Become fluent in your body's language. Listen and learn to discern the subtleties of its tone and the meaning of its phrases. If you must speak, speak kindly or speak not at all. Let your conversation be that of a close friend – intimate, honest, encouraging, and playful. But listen more than talk, observe and know.

What I know for sure is that yoga helps me return to myself, calling my mind home, making for a more peaceful, balanced, and healthier me. Yoga, with Expression and Spirit, brings the quiet deep into my being and into my bones. It is there that I tend the magic seeds of my authentic life. I wish this for you.

Yoga

Y is for Yoga

Confession: I am not a yoga purest.

I love yoga and am a certified Yoga Teacher but you will surely never ever see me on the cover of Yoga Journal. I do not aspire to Crow (Bakasana) or Wheel (Urdhva Dhanurasana). It is doubtful I will ever perfect my Boat pose (Navasana) as only one set of toes barely leaves the ground. I sometimes grunt impressively during Chaturanga Dandasana. And that is totally fine with me.

To be clear, I have a daily yoga practice, I teach yoga classes, and the Eight Limbs of Yoga are part of my daily life, informing the way I live. Nevertheless, my pressing focus is to feel grounded physically and mentally and to live mindfully in the present moment, fully in my body. Time on my mat, even 10-15 minutes, is one of my daily disciplines to live a healthy life. In that respect, my practice is impressive to precisely no one. In fact, I see it is a reprieve from impressing anyone, from a demanding world, and sometimes from a demanding me.

So much of life these days is about Performance (note the Capital P) or production, narrowly defined success measures and the bottom line. On my mat, however, nothing *needs* to happen that is measured by anyone else. My yoga practice is as much about simply rolling out my mat and listening carefully to what my body needs as it is about anything else, considering how I can genuinely care for myself as I move through my practice. On my mat, I return to the knowledge that I need not change a thing about myself to be whole and complete.

I remind my yoga students at the beginning of each class that everything I offer them is simply a suggestion. Once they have the basics, they are truly their best teachers. Listening to their physical and mental needs and responding in kind is far more important than anything else happening in the room.

Yes, yoga is one of my daily disciplines and it serves me well, but perhaps it feels foreign or daunting to you. Let's set that aside for a moment as I share with you a bit about a much-beloved class I taught for four years. It just might change the way you feel about yoga.

We simply called it 'Stretch and Bend.' No one had a mat. We all wore casual clothing and most everyone kept their shoes on. There were usually five or six of us and the average age was seventy or so. Not a single person would have self-identified as an athlete or athletic. We sat in chairs in a circle for 30-45 minutes every Monday evening.

Everyone participated fully to their ability doing poses modified from a studio class I also taught. We centered ourselves, practiced our diaphragmatic breathing, stretched and twisted, balanced, lengthened, strengthened, centered again, and then sat quietly for a minute or two. They loved the way they felt as they walked out the door, these mighty yogis, and I treasure all they taught me in our four years together.

Now back to you. Back to today. Back to this moment.

If you are curious about yoga, now is the time to find a Beginners or Intro class near you. Perhaps go meet the teacher before you show up for the first time. Ask questions! If you do not feel a connection or (heaven forbid) they appear disinterested in you or your needs, keep looking but start today. Get out of your own way and make that first yoga deposit in your life-long health account.

If you have your own practice but currently feel like a stranger to your mat, I invite you to dust it off now. Yes, now. I mean it. Go. If you do not have ten minutes for even a quick stretch, set your mat in a prominent place so you see it when you walk back in the door. The hardest part is simply rolling out your mat.

If you have not been to a class at your favorite studio or with your favorite teacher lately, by all means get thee to a studio! Just one class. No big promises necessary. Just today. Treat yourself. You are worth it.

What I know for sure is that yoga helps me return to myself and helps me call my mind home, making for a more peaceful, balanced, and healthy me. Yoga, with Expression and Spirit, helps me to be authentically me.

Do you hear it? Your mat is calling.

Collaboration Begins as an Inside Job

Collaboration is one of the finest, finest gifts of artistry. – *kd lang*

I was preparing for a meeting the other day about a collaborative venture, eager to explore the possibilities of a synergistic approach to a common interest. In preparation, I marshaled all the facts at my disposal, as well as my available tools and insights, then I made my lists. I gave thought to the skills, resources and experiences of the individuals involved noting how well they mesh and the power they bring when combined for possibilities far beyond the disparate pieces.

This is the very definition of collaboration, bringing together skills, ideas, tools, resources, insights and experiences in magical co-creation. Make room in the mix for a bit of mystery and – voila – a new and remarkable something comes into being!

Upon further reflection, I came to understand that collaboration is not simply an outward, logistical combining of the efforts of two or more people. For me, collaboration begins inside, as part of my inner work. My daily yoga practice involves aligning my attention, breath and body for a few minutes as often as possible. Rather than compartmentalizing my physical efforts as distinct from my mental or emotional efforts, I choose to practice weaving them together on my yoga mat. This full collaboration of my mind and body brings me back to the fullness of myself, all resources at the ready. Resourceful and alive.

Believe me, I know this is not always easy.

In today's distracted, planning-for-the-future or living-in-the-past world, it requires discipline to bring ourselves fully present to this moment. Now and here. If you are like me, it is more common than I care to admit to look up and realize that twenty minutes have passed. Poof. Gone. Nothing constructive accomplished or gained, no real enjoyment or value, precious moments squandered.

I recognize that when my attention is fragmented or far away from the present moment, my mind and body are not collaborating and my best resources are diminished. Like a skilled athlete who consciously ties one arm behind her back or hops on one leg, distraction is an unnecessary if not purposeful handicap. In that context, it sounds ridiculous, doesn't it? Who would intentionally sabotage themself in such a significant way?

And yet, disconnection and distraction are rampant.

Science shows us that the brain is far less efficient when we multi-task. Yet, the impact of multi-tasking plays out in nearly every aspect of our daily, common lives. From distracted driving, work-place inefficiencies, relationships without depth, to poor workmanship, a lack of focus peppers nearly every aspect of common life.

So what is the anecdote?

Focus. Being present here and now. Mindful attention. But, ask yourself honestly, can you actually do this anymore? It can feel daunting to commit to doing just one thing at a time or not doing anything at all for even a few moments each day. I certainly find it challenging but infinitely worth the effort. A yoga mat is my learning laboratory on which I practice.

In a previous chapter, I wrote about the skills and tools I believe will distinguish leaders in the future. Specifically, calm, focus, attention, listening and self-awareness. As I read the headlines and move through my day, I am more convinced than ever that we are collectively losing the mental muscles of focus and attention. These vital tools are being replaced by empty numbing, surrendering our discernment and self-control to whomever yells the loudest, to all the shiny objects, and to the latest addiction – the perpetual scroll.

Does it really matter? What is the toll?

In our numbing and distraction, we unconsciously give away precious pieces of our very lives. In addition, our relationship with self suffers, as do our relationships with others, our ability to solve problems, our ability to think critically, and to think for ourselves.

Do you ever get wrapped around the axle about something? You know what I mean. Your brain is like a hamster on a wheel, your gut is in impressive knots, you cannot sleep, your inner dialog never stops and it all looks dark?

Or perhaps you are noticing that you spend much of your time on autopilot with your mind miles away while the body scurries about. Numbing, numbing, numbing...

Here is what I am learning (and re-learning):

Take a deep breath. And then another. Notice the coolness as the breath enters the body. Notice the warmth as it leaves. Bring your mind back to this moment. And this moment. And this moment too.

This is your life. This moment. This breath. Here. Now.

I believe we are at our most resourceful when the mind, the body and the breath collaborate together in this moment. The past, which cannot be changed, is firmly where it belongs. The future, which is entirely unknown, is yet to arrive. Our challenge is to live in this moment, here and now, in your body, and fully experience what this moment has to teach you, all of your resources at the ready, fully resourceful. At its finest, this is yoga.

The worries of the day will not magically be resolved if we are present to them and, frankly, there might be pain. When we are present in body, mind, and breath, however, we unite our immediate resources to function as one. We are fully alive to meet each challenge.

It is time to reclaim our best inner resources. As we begin the great inner collaboration, we bring focus and attention to the present moment. As we marshal our strengths, our unique gifts and our many resources, we come face-to-face with our life and are asked to choose to be an active participant.

How do we begin?

Look up and look around.

Take a breath, then take another.

Notice your surroundings. Feel your body in the space you occupy. Notice your thoughts. Be still for a moment. Be, here and now. Lend your attention to the symphony of the present moment, your energy a lovely note in the orchestra of life.

This is your life. This moment. This breath. Claim it! See it. Bring your whole self to it.

Listening Deeply and Responding Kindly

My dogs are barking.

My back is singing.

My belly is grumbling.

The body is always talking, rarely at a loss for something to say. Even the language we use to describe our physical sensations is verbal in nature. We have an innate understanding that the body is communicating all the time. And the body, like a child, is always trying to get our attention. It sends signals, both subtle and loud, whether we are awake or asleep, in an attempt to tell us about our well-being.

Are you listening? Or have you turned a deaf ear? Do you know the language of your body? Can you understand what it is saying? Taking this one step further, do you have the tools you need to respond to your body in a kind and healthy way?

I spent more than forty years disconnected from my body, namely my right hip and leg. I had my first reconstructive hip surgery at the age of eleven months followed by nearly two years in casts from my waist to my toes, the result of severe congenital hip dysplasia. Other than walking a little funny and not being able to sit cross-legged, I never paid much attention to my hip or the signals it sent me. In my twenties, however, my hip had deteriorated and I could no longer walk. The pain was excruciating and I could no longer ignore it.

At age twenty-eight, I had a hip replacement. By the time I was in my late forties I learned that more than one-half of the bone bed in the right side of my pelvis was worn away, leading to another hip surgery and the rebuilding of that section of my pelvis. Prior to my last surgery, I was so disconnected from the signals my body tried to send me, I still walked a few miles every day and kept up all of my activities. I limped through my life, mystified when people asked if I was okay.

My pain threshold was utterly out of whack, living each day with pre-verbal learned responses to pain that began as an infant. I mentioned to my walking partner one day that I was in a bit of discomfort and considering taking an over-the-counter pain medication, something I had never used and knew nothing about. With her vast knowledge of such things, she schooled me on various available remedies, such as ibuprofen, Tylenol, aspirin, and Aleve. Then she asked me to rate my pain on a scale one to ten.

"Oh, pretty consistently about a seven," was my matter of fact response. "Spiking to nine, like just a few minutes ago as we came around that last curve."

"Seven?! Nine?!" she exclaimed. "Really? I reach for the ibuprofen at about a two or three."

It was evident that my pain threshold was on the fritz and I was deeply disconnected from my right hip and leg. Rather than tending to myself, I ignored my hip and even shamed it with my inner thoughts. (*Keep up! Keep moving!*) The grooves of this pattern were deep, well-worn and old. These patterns ruled without filter or supervision – the dictator of my inner world. I soldiered on unaware, living primarily in my mind and ignoring my body.

A common theme from students in my yoga and meditation classes is the significant amount of time we spend these days living in our heads. Thoughts run amok, racing and whirling, rumination rules, and mindless numbing occupy a significant amount of our mental energy. We spend so much time living in our heads that we ignore the signals from the body, no longer fluent in its language and out of practice listening with few skills to respond in a kind and meaningful way.

For some, the only communication with the body is old, programmed and unkind, deeply ingrained habits further deepened by our perpetual screen time. (The disconnectedness resulting from all our connectedness.) A yoga student once shared a story about the day she realized she was her own worst enemy. In a moment of clarity, she heard herself speak to her body more unkindly and harshly than anyone else in her life. As she tuned into her beliefs about her body and appearance, she knew she would never allow someone so speak to her (or to anyone) in the way she mentally spoke to herself.

How then do we reconnect with the body, become aware of our inner dialog, learn the body's language, and develop a healthy dialog with kind and caring responses? For me the answer is Yoga, the first thread in a triple-braided cord of authentic living. Yoga provides a space and the tools to listen and respond.

Yoga continues to provide me with powerful tools to deepen my relationship with my body. Each time I step on my mat, I experience what I have come to know as the two sides of myself. Early on, as I developed a yoga practice, I became aware of my feelings of frustration with and even shame about my right side, the weakness, deformity, and limitations of my hip and leg. I also became aware of the great pride I felt about the strength of my left side which was muscular, flexible, and adept, compensating for the other side all of my life. On my mat I became aware that this dichotomy was not only physically visible, it also spilled over into the way I saw myself and the world.

Off the yoga mat and out in the world, I began to notice how I used my hip as currency. I had repeated the story of my hip surgeries and years of body casts thousands of times to impress, for sympathy, and as an excuse. My hip saga was a string I plucked often, a song I knew well. I consciously and unconsciously used it to my advantage.

On my mat, I began to hear the loud persistent inner dialog, the ping-pong between left and right, anger and pride. With time, I became fluent in this language, becoming consciously aware of bodily signals that I had ignored for most of my life. My yoga practice became a learning laboratory and the perfect practice space for developing a collaborative and kind relationship between my body and my mind.

As I dove deeper into my yoga experience, my old patterns became hugely evident and painfully unavoidable. My old story no longer rang true and it was evident that it was keeping me stuck. The currency didn't have the same buying power it used to and was far less satisfying. This deeper awareness called for something new. The tools of yoga provided me with awareness as well as kind and thoughtful physical responses to what my body really needed.

With awareness, inner fluency, and yoga postures as tools, I continue daily to transform my inner and outer worlds by unifying my body and mind, by weaving together the two inner sides of myself, by releasing the old stories, and by learning new responses to my body's pressing needs. As a result, I feel healthy, alive and whole.

Are you ready to reconnect with your body? Is it time to become fluent in your inner native tongue? Does your tool kit have room for body-mind alignment? Are you ready to begin?

Healing the Inner Divide

Kindness begins at home. – *Rick Hanson, Ph.D.*

She was beautiful. Her smile was warm and kind and she moved like a gazelle. After two decades as a runner, she was lean and light, seemingly always on the move, fresh from a shower, and smartly dressed. By all outward appearances, she had it all. And yet here she was, deeply unsettled and seeking support. You see, she was at war. Inside her most-beautiful self, a punishing unkindness was sapping her of joy and impacting her biology.

For years she ran and raced and won. One entire closet was filled with trophies and ribbons, abundant evidence of her skill and speed. Her body performed amazing feats as she propelled herself like a mythical winged creature. For her, however, it was never enough. She was always reaching but never clasping. Despite the many trophies and the runner's high, she finished each race certain that she had somehow missed the mark. Recently she had begun to feel deeply unsettled, unable to find peace or experience joy. She felt divided inside, at war with herself. Using the following three steps, we set out together to heal the inner divide.

Step One – Think Kind Thoughts. Our first step together was to sharpen her awareness of her mental body (her thoughts and emotions) and develop her tools of neutral observation, simply noticing without judgement. Using yoga as our tool, we began to practice together while looking in a large floor-to-ceiling mirror. As we practiced basic yoga postures, holding them for several breaths, I asked her to listen to her thoughts, to tune into her inner voice. Initially, she had no idea what I was talking about so we moved to a gentler posture and continued to breathe. With additional prompting, she began to verbalize her thoughts, giving voice to the dialog going on inside her head.

She was certain she was not doing the posture correctly and her breathing was all wrong. Her hamstrings were not cooperating, her outfit was outdated and she was ashamed that she could not reach her toes. These thoughts recycled over and over as she pushed and reached and grunted and gasped.

"I'm so mean to myself!" she cried as she listened to her thoughts. "Not just mean but downright cruel!" After a long pause she murmured, "I sound just like Coach and I'm not even running."

I asked her to ease up a bit in her posture, to stop pushing, and to relax, bringing her focus to her breath. Inhale. Exhale. Iiiiiinnnhaaaale. Exxxxhaaaaale. After a few moments of quiet and several deep breaths, the tears began to flow.

Through her tears she clearly recognized the voice of her earliest coach, a surrogate father figure, someone she desperately wanted to please. She ran and ran, but Coach never provided healthy encouragement and always pushed for more. Whatever she did, it was never enough. Decades later, Coach was long gone but his punishing dialog still punctuated each foot fall and pushed her to exhaustion. She was still reaching but never clasping. Many years later, she was still not enough.

Together we shaped a new self-dialog, a script of neutral and kind words she spoke to herself daily, infused with encouragement. She not only repeated this new language as she ran but also spent time meditating on how she would feel if she knew that her kinder script was in fact true. This way of interacting with herself was foreign and uncomfortable for quite some time, but she persisted until eventually this inner banter became her natural way of thinking. With a new appreciation for her body, she began to listen more closely to what she needed and took better care of herself as well. On her yoga mat, she integrated a far kinder relationship with, and a gentler response to, her physical self.

Step Two – Be Kind to The Body. With a kinder inner banter, she continued her yoga practice, deepening her awareness of her physical body. Where her relationship with her body had long been only about 'More!' and 'Faster!', time on her yoga mat taught her about listening and adapting. She began to realize that the fullest expression of her yoga postures could sometimes be found in easing back a bit, not pushing, being kind to her body, and finding peace in the pose.

As she listened more closely to her physical needs, she cut back on her running schedule and dedicated more time to rest and nourishment, ease and self-care. After years of running with a concerned expression and deeply furrowed brow, she began to smile as she ran and to delight in the beauty of her surroundings. She no longer ate simply to improve her race times, she began to taste her food and delight in the aromas, feeling deep gratitude for the ability to nourish her body.

Step Three – Be Here Now. As she released the voices of the past and listened to her body, she began to spend more time in the present moment, right here and now. She no longer felt constantly chased and berated, always reaching for what was illusive. When she ran, it was no longer about chasing the unattainable or pleasing someone else. She now ran for the joy of it, for the wondrous abilities of her physical body, for the peace running brought her, and for the opportunity to enjoy the beauty of her surroundings. Running was transformed from a form of punishment to a moving meditation. In this transformation, she found joy.

Today's Outer World and the Inner Divide.

For too many of us, our inner world reflects the media-driven divided outer world. TVs blare non-stop stories and images designed to incite, ignite, infuriate and divide. Our gadget-obsession dumps a steady stream of drama, unkindness and unpleasantness into our consciousness without filter. As we give all our waking attention to fighting, tragedy, blaming, and dividing, we bring it all inward, unconsciously drawing the battle inside. We swim daily between ruminating on a past that cannot be changed or projecting an imagined future that has not yet arrived, devoid of resources to filter and protect. None of this noise has the ability to improve our lives, yet we continue to scroll, post, numb, ruminate, share, and project. As a result, we are rarely present to the NOW, the only opportunity we have to actively heal the brokenness and create what we truly want.

And Now the Good News.

As humans, by design, we are made to heal. Every cell is programmed for growth and healing. We are extraordinarily resilient and creative when we choose to treat the body kindly. When we harness our inner dialog and bring our awareness to the present, we take back the reigns and set our own course. Uniting the body and mind through our breath and awareness, we bring together our greatest resources. By uniting our whole selves with the neutral, non-judging present moment, we can observe and see clearly, making a space for a new reality and for what is possible.

Healing the inner divide is a worthwhile endeavor requiring your attention, awareness, patience, and persistence. As we reshape our inner dialog, re-frame our relationship with the body, and re-commit daily to spending time in the present, we knit together the disconnected broken pieces and heal our warring parts.

Elizabeth Cabalka

Expression

The Puzzle

If you bring forth what is within you, what you bring forth will save you. If you do not bring forth what is within you, what you do not bring forth will destroy you. *—The Gospel of Thomas*

"How do you write a book?" she asked.

I love that question and I imagine the path for this particular form of self-expression is different from writer to writer. While writing this book, I found that my process was akin to working on a 10,000 piece puzzle without benefit of the guiding image on the lid of the box.

In February 2015, in a funk, I recognized that the large and cumbersome package filled with my burdens and many questions that I had begrudgingly lugged around for years was actually a cleverly wrapped gift. When I awoke to this fact, I paused to inspect the wrapping which was torn to reveal a simply adorned box. Casting aside the wrapping, I clearly saw the cover on which my wisest self long ago scribbled in crayon, *'Open Me Now, Elizabeth! It is time.'*

Holed up in the darkened bedroom on a gloriously sunny Arizona Sunday afternoon, I upended the box and looked curiously at the contents that tumbled out in a messy pile on the bed. Puzzle pieces! Scads of them! More than I could count. Another look at the box cover confirmed there was no guiding image. Nothing. Zilch. What a conundrum.

In an angsty little snit, I kicked the figurative pile aside. And then my world changed when **Y**oga **E**xpression **S**pirit showed up in my journal. My gazed moved from the newly arrived tantalizing nugget in my journal to the pile of puzzle pieces and the discarded box with a message from myself.

And then I knew....

This pile of bits, this collection of the many pieces of my life to date, paired with my new insights, would become my next book – **Y**oga **E**xpression **S**pirit – which you now hold in your hands.

For over a year, I busily worked on this puzzle. I turned all the pieces upright, located the edges, and even assembled most of the frame. Then I set about the hard work of assembling the inner image.

This is what it is like to write a book. In this case, I found that the absence of a guiding image on the box cover provided space for vast amounts of creativity. My guiding image came from within not from atop a cardboard box.

What you may not know is that I am not a full-time writer. While my day-time focus is squarely rooted in work and family, I spend precious creative moments in the wee early hours, after dinner dishes are done, and on weekends giving voice and expression to my authentic self. As the wonderful and wise author, Elizabeth Gilbert, urges in one of her Big Magic podcasts, I sneak off daily and have a hot and sweaty affair with my creativity.

You see, I simply have to do this. My authentic life depends on allowing my inner self expression. My well-being depends on it. My very happiness depends on it. And, in some not-unimportant way, the world depends on it.

I have come to know that our authentic inner nudgings, when unexpressed, are not benign. Now in my fifties, it is no longer acceptable to ignore my authentic self and leave things undone. To do so would be an act most unkind, even cruel. Regarding kindness as I do as deeply important in this world, this self-cruelty will no longer do. So, create I must, each and every day, as an act of self-care.

Therefore, I have written this book and assembled the many pieces. The process was messy, joyful, rewarding, wildly creative, and deeply satisfying. I am grateful you have joined me to explore the results. Please do not let it stop here in these pages. While you may not feel the need to write a book, there *is* most certainly something within you that is seeking expression. What is that something? By all means, stop ignoring it! Your authentic life depends on it. Your well-being depends on it. Your very happiness depends on it. And, in some important way, the world depends on it too.

Inside Out

That's okay, honey. You're just not all that creative. – *Crochet Instructor, circa 1974*

I was ten years old. It was Saturday afternoon and I was one of five students in a crochet class at Stitchville USA. As I jammed my incomprehensible pile of knots into my jacket pocket along with all my frustrations, I also unknowingly closed the door on an understanding of myself. I believed the teacher's words, I was not creative. The evidence was in a tangled mess in my pocket. Surely she knew creative from not. Apparently I was not.

Honestly, I am not sure what she actually said that day. Simply a poorly-executed-but-well-intended attempt to provide comfort and ease my frustration I suspect. The hard, knotty evidence in my pocket, however, paired with her few words shaped what I decided about myself and what I continued to believe for another twenty years.

This formative experience is commonly called an Art Scar. They are often acquired at a young age and the depth of the damage beneath the Art Scar can be sizeable. For many of us with Art Scars, deeply-buried Art Shame is attached to the formative experience and remains as actively at work beneath our experiences today as the day it first lodged in our consciousness. While you may not readily recall the specifics of the experience, you may have an automatic knee-jerk response to even the suggestion of anything creative. "Creative? Ooooh, nooo-ooo-ooo. Not me. I am *not* creative. Make something? Nope. I can't. Not gonna' happen." This is often followed by the ever-popular, "I cannot even draw a stick figure."

They are prevalent, these art scars, yet I am still surprised when I find them in others. Years ago one of my coaching clients was a successful business woman and brilliant strategist. Her ability to visualize and communicate a unique solution to a complex problem was widely acknowledged. When she attended one of my retreats, however, she dug in her heels when it came to participating in a simple craft project related to the weekend's theme. She announced loudly and often that she was simply not creative and would have to find another way to occupy the next ninety minutes. There was no convincing her otherwise. She was averse to even touching the craft supplies and fled the room.

A friend and I were discussing this topic recently and she mentioned her shared similar long-held belief. She was also apparently not creative. It wasn't until her mother commended her fearless creativity with food and entertaining, repeatedly trying new things with curiosity and flair, that she opened to the possibility that maybe she was creative after all.

For over three decades, a dear friend has delighted in telling me about the meals he creates, the colors, the smells, the flavors, and each ingredient. I have enjoyed dissertations on home-made stew with the tiny little ears of corn and too many pot-roasts to count. Food is his palette and he is quite the artist, though he would positively implode if I called him creative.

Too often 'creativity' is assigned only to artists in the traditional sense, namely those who paint,

73

weave, craft or sculpt. And only to those who do these things well, the professional. This is unfortunate and also false. Creativity is our nature from our first breath to our last. It is within each of us in one form or another but far too often is quashed or suppressed to our detriment.

'E' is for Expression

I remember that day my limiting, non-creative view of myself changed. The filter I had firmly secured over my vision for two decades fell away and the door to my creativity blasted wide open. In fact, the door nearly flew right off its hinges.

I was attending a Women's Retreat and we had arrived at the appointed time for the obligatory craft project. My ten-year-old self in a thirty-year-old body had dawdled a bit, dreading the moment that my lack of creativity would be exposed. I was one of the last to enter the room where everyone was working, chattering, happy, and busily making. Clearly these people were creative! Soon they would know I was not.

I tentatively approached a table covered in one-foot square upholstery samples mounded nearly three feet high in every conceivable color and pattern. As

I looked around at these happy women engaged in making and joyfully playing, my hands unconsciously dug deep into the piles of fabric. The colors and textures triggered a sensory marvel. Before I knew it, my arms were buried up to the elbows in fabric and something within me stirred.

One hour later, I had created a journal covered in a beautiful floral textured weave and I loved it dearly. The corners were uneven and there was an unplanned glob of hot glue on the back cover but it was mine, of me, through me, and I came alive.

In the months that followed I purchased a glue gun of my very own and made ten similar journals for my family and friends. As I think back, I was the quintessential elementary child with something for everyone's refrigerator. Two decades of Art Shame fell away. Creative expression poured through me. The dam was broken and I could not create enough.

In the last twenty years, I have dabbled in decoupage, water colors, sewing, gardening, writing, singing, and cooking with fearless abandon. Some might add reckless, like that year I learned to play the fiddle. Some of it has been perfectly awful (again, fiddle) and some of it has pretty darn good, but that matters not a whit. It is the act of making, the expression of something within me coming to life, which somehow nourishes me and calms my mind.

What about you? What have you decided about your creativity? How long have you held that belief? Are you ready to acknowledge your art scars and set them aside just for a little while, at least long enough to try something new? What is it that has been calling to you? Your garden? An essay? Your kitchen? A dance class? A bird house? An instrument? A foreign language? A paint brush? What is that spark of creativity within you that is seeking expression through you, yearning to come out to play?

What say you, my fellow wounded maker? Shall we claim our art scars now as the tuition for our creative learning? To suppress that creative spark is not benign. If for no other reason than your well-being, let your creativity flow!

Please make, express or do something today – *anything* – for the pleasure of no one but yourself, just because you can.

The Power of Uncomfortable

You will either step forward into growth or you will step back into safety. – *Abraham Maslow*

I was twenty-five years old with a budding idea about becoming a professional writer and speaker. The idea was pretty new but it felt delicious and compelling. Just a crazy dream but one that would not let me go.

Our church hosted Soup Suppers at the time during Lent, a gathering for a simple meal after which a church member shared a bit of their personal story. I decided this would be my debut and signed up for week #3. I was certain this would be perfect.

My hair was beautifully coiffed, my best suit was freshly cleaned with an Ascot in the pocket of the red suit jacket. My jewelry, make-up, and shoes were polished and perfect. Damn, I looked good. I had written and rewritten my remarks, now neatly typed, double spaced, neatly arranged in a folder. I had practiced several times and I was ready!

I do not remember much about the Soup or the Supper but I'll tell you what I do remember. Vividly. The Flop Sweat! I was so nervous that the sweat was running into the waist-band of my navy blue skirt. My adorable suit jacket was now two-toned with deep red sweat stained side panels from my armpits to waist and down my arms approaching my wrists. My makeup was smeared because my face was perspiring and I had blotted it one too many times.

At the appointed time, my sweaty-self wobbled up to the podium, opened my folder to my prepared remarks, took a deep breath, and opened my mouth. *Gack.* Nothing came out. I tried again and emitted a feeble *squawk* followed closely by an impressive dry-mouthed *cluck.* Apparently the previous perspiration was just a little preview because the flood gates opened and I was now dripping on the floor.

Twelve minutes later, I somehow finished my remarks and fled to the back of the fellowship hall, arms pinned to my sides in an attempt to cover my drenched jacket. While people were kind in their comments, I think they felt just as mortified as I felt. They had witnessed a train wreck. The one silver lining was that this was a gentle crowd – my tribe – and several of them were my baby-sitters when I was an infant. Thankfully they threw nothing as I spoke, though I would not have blamed them one little bit had they heckled, tossed a roll or pitched a butter patty my way in protest.

A mentor of mine approached after most of the crowd left.

"So, how was that?" he asked with a playful grin. "Still want to be a speaker and writer?" He stared intently at my red face then continued. "If you really want this, Elizabeth, are you willing to keep doing this, even badly, until you can do it well?"

I had to seriously think about that one but not for long.

Doggone it, yes! I wanted this! Not this misery but the dream. I knew that what I wanted was waiting on the other side of all the deep discomfort and embarrassment. In that exchange, my mentor helped me form a new relationship with uncomfortable and, twenty-seven years later, that lesson continues to inform my life.

For this reason I believe that feeling uncomfortable can be a very good thing. In fact, I believe feeling uncomfortable is an important step in the process of conscious growth because uncomfortable shows us the edges of our world. We have become so averse, however, to anything that requires even a whiff of uncomfortable that we stay stuck right where we are, weeping and wailing about how miserable we feel yet utterly unwilling to make a change. The complaining is familiar. Choosing what is known, the comfortably uncomfortable, instead of the rich and fertile uncomfortable is often where we live. Comfortably uncomfortable, numb and stuck.

But here is the cool part about actively choosing uncomfortable: We are never as close to that new 'something' we are seeking than when we are deeply uncomfortable and choose to press forward anyway. In the process we learn that uncomfortable is temporary and does not last forever.

Let's unpack the journey through uncomfortable in the following four steps.

Step One – Captive. There was a time in my life when I allowed my conditioned thinking to rule my life. I did not question my thoughts or ideas. The latest shiny object gathered all my attention and the good opinion of others caused me to twist into unrecognizable shapes. I was doing what I was *supposed* to do, living someone else's idea of my life, feeling unhappy but that was known and familiar. My life was not my own but I knew no other way of being. My everyday conditioned thoughts created conditioned feelings which created conditioned results. I did not really feel fully alive but at least my life felt familiar.

Step Two – Reason. Over time I began to wonder if there might be a different way of living, perhaps even living fully in a way that felt compelling. What if I stepped out of my programmed, conditioned little world and tried something different? I gave serious thought to some new ideas about who I wanted to be and what I might create for my life. Encounters with people, books, speakers, and ideas started to rattle my cage and caused me to ponder. Ideas that felt utterly audacious would not leave my thoughts. Write a book?! Become a teacher? Lead workshops and retreats? Wot?! That's crazy. But, then again, what if...? These ideas rolled around inside me for a good long time as I continued on with my same ol' life, thinking the same ol' conditioned thoughts, feeling the same ol' conditioned feelings, moving through the same ol' conditioned actions, still creating the same ol' conditioned results. No action yet, just a lot of thinking. Even so, this step was important in shaping my new vision.

Step Three – Uncomfortable. The day I started to take action toward my hopes and dreams, when I no longer simply hoped and wished, I felt both exhilarated but also afraid! And uncomfortable. Each new action took me out of my conditioned life and set up new and unfamiliar feelings. For me, unfamiliar meant uncomfortable. This is where I impatience previously caused me to abandon my dreams and step back into safety, choosing the known over the necessary and glorious uncomfortable that could move me toward my dreams. Out to the edge of possible I raced, then beat a hasty retreat back to safety. Out and back, out and back. Until one day I decided to remain out there in uncomfortable and press forward anyway.

Step Four – Freedom. Twenty-seven years ago I chose uncomfortable and it led me repeatedly to freedom. Pressing against the edges of my world, choosing the pathways through uncomfortable, led me to freedom and to my authentic life. While I have been deeply uncomfortable at times (and even failed miserably a time or two), the gift of persistence has produced three books, over 600 teaching and speaking gigs, and the realization of countless other wild dreams to boot. More importantly, however, against all odds, I am gratefully living that crazy dream that came to me almost three decades ago with just enough lingering flop sweat to keep me humble.

I believe deep in my bones that there is something waiting for *you* on the other side of uncomfortable. I encourage you to trade a measure of comfort for a bit of uncomfortable. It is absolutely worth it. Next time you feel a rich and robust uncomfortable, consider acknowledging it for what it is – the pathway to the possible! Stay with it! Breathe into it. Lean forward and breathe through it.

Allow yourself to feel uncomfortable for a while on the way to a new you. Uncomfortable is temporary. Hang in there. You are not alone. You've got this. I promise.

Elizabeth Cabalka

LOL

'LOL', a friend texted as we sipped our coffee.

I watched as his fingers automatically shared a message of joy and mirth when in reality he was grimacing with both mental and physical pain. My friend was clearly not **L**aughing **O**ut **L**oud, despite the little cha-cha of his fingers on his phone.

I gently pointed out this discrepancy and he was somewhat taken aback. He showed me the adorable photo he received from a friend. The baby was dressed in a funny outfit which was certainly grin-worthy, but why the LOL when it did not reflect his real response and his actual state of being?

"When was the last time you actually laughed out loud?" I asked. He just shrugged.

I probed further, asking how often this occurred. He didn't even pause to think. "It's constant. All the time, but doesn't everybody do it? It's kind of expected." He paused, then added, "What's the big deal anyway?"

This may seem like mountain-out-of-a-mole-hill thinking and, if this incident was isolated or unique, I would agree. This text and his response, however, represented one of hundreds of instances that daily widened the crevasse between his real experience of life and the highly edited image he projected to the world.

It's just a little LOL so what is the big deal?

I believe this *is* a big deal. In fact, for me, it is a great big hairy wildly important all too often ignored socially accepted health depleting joy sucking honest to goodness great big deal. When we choose to LOL our days and nights away, we are more likely to experience depression, anxiety, feelings of helplessness, and disconnectedness. That is the big deal. That is why this matters.

The Authentic Personality

A brilliant 2008 study called The Authentic Personality[1] beautifully illuminates precisely why

LOL-mania and our growing number of disconnected interactions are a big deal and something about which we should care deeply if we want to live authentically and live well.

The 2008 study correlated the impact of the following three factors on our individual well-being and self-esteem.

Self-Alienation, represented by the experience of not knowing oneself or feeling out of touch with one-self.

Authentic Living, being true to oneself in most situations and living in accordance with one's values and beliefs.

Accepting external influences, the extent to which one accepts the influence of other people and the belief that one has to conform to the expectations of others.

While these three factors have long been considered interrelated, the 2008 study showed how these factors are also equally important to individual well-being.

Here are just six of the many questions researchers asked study participants. As you read these questions, consider how closely each statement reflects your life. In fact, read each question aloud and notice your physical and mental response.

- I don't know how I really feel inside.

- I feel cut off from who I really am.

- I have to hide the way I feel inside.

- I feel pressured to behave in certain ways.

- I usually laugh because other people are laughing.

- I make my own choices in life.

Did one or more of these questions cause you to squirm? There are a few on that list that make me squirm as I consider the amount of time I spend engaged in actions or thoughts that disconnect me from my authentic self. You too?

The Big 'So-What'

I challenge you to reclaim your authentic life with your next LOL. More specifically, what if LOL only showed up in your electronic communications if you really, truly, honest-to-Pete, *did* in fact laugh out loud?

Begin to notice the number of times you weigh in with a LOL or an emoticon that in no way represents you, your thoughts or your emotions. What would happen if you paused for a moment, then genuinely responded with real, full, meaningful words. Or not! What would happen if you didn't respond at all?

If you feel compelled to respond, try picking up the phone for a real conversation. Better yet, power down the phone and talk to the person sitting next to you. Even better yet, power down the phone and go for a walk with the person next to you. Become engaged in the world around you, engaged in a way that really reflects the authentic you.

Take the first step: if you are not feelin' it, do *not* send it! Your well-being and self-esteem depend on it.

FOOTNOTE:
(1)The Authentic Personality: A Theoretical and Empirical Conceptualization and the Development of the Authenticity Scale; Journal of Counseling Psychology Copyright 2008 by the American Psychological Association, 2008, Vol. 55, No. 3, 385–3992008, Vol. 55, No. 3, 385–399

Busy

"Busy is dumb."

So says Tony Crabbe in his terrific book simply titled **Busy**(2). **Busy** is not only ineffective, the author states, but it is also the leading contributor to stress. For that reason alone, **Busy** can also be wildly unhealthy.

The physical toll of **Busy**-induced prolonged stress is well-known and includes anxiety, depression, memory deficits, emotional instability, irritability, sleep disruption, road rage, heartburn, back aches, neck aches, body aches, suppressed immune function, high blood pressure and a racing heart. **Busy** isn't just annoying and it is certainly not benign. **Busy**, especially **Busy-Without-End,** can be harmful and even deadly. This is certainly not news. **Busy** is rampant!

I look at **Busy** a little differently. I experience **Busy** as a state of mind, especially noticeable when I become disconnected and mindless, a victim to my schedule. At the same time, I believe it is possible to live a deliciously full life without feeling a smidge of **Busy**. Consciously choosing how to fill our days and how to spend our energy then remaining present to each experience we create can lead to a full and rewarding existence. Very different than **Busy**.

Interestingly, when I feel most **Busy**, I am tempted to incessantly and mindlessly pile on even more **Busy,** filling every available space with the mental noise of **Digital Busy**. There is this curious itch (or shall I say addiction?) to fill every space between the **Busy** with a few texts, checking my email, a quick google search or scanning Facebook. This turns **Busy** into **BUSY**.

Sadly, not only are we collectively **BUSY** but we are also seemingly addicted to the **BUSY**. Digital noise is the cross-generational addiction of our time. One friend recently admitted that she knew she was hopelessly addicted to her phone when she misplaced it, triggering an all-out panic attack. Without a doubt, we are busy, but we are the ones creating all the **BUSY** and this is good news, albeit cleverly disguised. If we are creating it, we can change it.

When my life reached a crisis point, I began a conscious study of how I was spending my energy each day. I looked closely at my schedule noting that my days were filled with a combination of *have to* and mindless activity, these taking precedence over purposeful, meaningful living.

I also began to notice my thoughts. My habitual negative thoughts and monkey-mind-wanderings were clearly having their way with me. And what about the spaces in between my activities? There was no stillness or silence.

Perhaps this resonates with you. In a moment of quiet, I reach for the phone, swipe open a screen, tap on an app, scroll, scroll, scroll. Just like that, ten minutes are gone. *Poof*

What is the result of filling *all* of the spaces with **Digital Busy**? One minute here, two there, five, ten, and more. We are trading away our very lives with each filled-up space! Each instance or moment may not feel significant but add them up and they are impressive and disheartening.

Those spare moments to linger, wonder, ponder, and savor are almost extinct, gobbled up by unconscious consumption. Junk food for the brain. Munch, munch, munch, scroll, scroll, and scroll. Those few moments of non-doing (long ago called boredom or idleness), in which we previously dialed the pressure down a notch, have become most evident in their absence, swallowed whole by nothing taking with them a momentary reprieve.

With this in mind, let's allow for spaces once again. Spaces to live, not simply observe. Your life may be no less full but the spaces in-between will no longer be jammed with the unnecessary and non-critical. A moment of non-doing that recently triggered aimless scrolling can contain calming deep breaths or (gasp) nothing at all. One minute at a time, begin to notice the real, live world around you and see your real self in it.

Why bother, you ask? What is the payoff?

When I began a practice of allowing spaces, I returned to myself and to my authentic life. Beauty returned to the forefront of my awareness. In fact, to my surprise I was swimming in beauty, not simply viewing the photos of someone else's experience of beauty. Challenges were present too, but at least I was present to them, not simply numb. Perhaps most importantly, over time **BUSY** became **Busy** became busy became fully-alive.

The spaces in-between can hold all manner of richness. Marvelous mysteries, important insights, challenges, self-care opportunities, discussions, noticing, relationships, and beauty. Our lives are not simply lived in the grand gestures and the goals but also in the spaces, the delicious in-between.

What about you? Are you ready to turn **BUSY** into **Busy,** or maybe even busy? Or are you ready to go all-in, ditching busy entirely? Start small, just one moment at a time, and see what you notice in the quiet still spaces in-between.

FOOTNOTE:
(2) Busy - How to Thrive in a World of Too Much, by Tony Crabbe; US Edition 2014, Grand Central Publishing.

Elizabeth Cabalka

Life Making in Five Steps

The only thing more important than your to-do list is your to-be list. The only thing more important than your to-be list is to be. *– Alan Cohen*

I am a List Maker.

In fact, I am a list maker descended from gifted Palmer-script list makers. I become bereft and a bit directionless without a list. Truth be told, I have been known to create lists of things I already did just for the satisfaction of crossing them off.

Lists order my days, my life, and my dreams. I also love schedules. Oh, a good schedule supported by a list makes me nearly tingly. Self-care rituals make the list as well, such as meditation and a daily walk.

Lists serve me in many ways. If it is on the list, it gets my attention. In a world of much (often too much) that pulls at my attention and demands my energy, the list guides me and helps keep me focused. Lists allow me to prioritize and keep the emotion out of whether or not something gets done. "I don't feel like it" is not the deciding factor because, well, it is on the list. Lists are part of my daily discipline, like a personal secretary in the art of making my life. My lists have long helped manifest my day-to-day life as well as numerous all-consuming, great big, crazy, wild dreams.

As with many things, however, I recently realized that the list is a wonderful servant but a horrible master. With this realization, my beloved list has become just one item in a far more expansive creative process of Life Making. I have reframed the list as a valuable and effective tool, but one of many, a cog in the wheel with its rightful place.

A wise friend and I were comparing notes recently about the process of life making, how we each bring our authentic selves and our dreams forth in tangible expressions, large and small, each day. The outcome of that conversation is a five-step process for life making and the art of authentic living.

Step One – Clear a Space.

Meditation, the ability to cultivate inner quiet, anchors us to the present moment and allows us to listen deeply. If you are like me, you may initially hear nothing but the loud and cluttered mind scampering and screaming, drowning out everything else. But, with meditation and mindfulness tools and a bit of patience, we can dial down the volume on the craziness until we can hear our deeper and quieter inner voice.

One technique I find helpful is to imagine a white board filled with notes, thoughts, lists, and ideas, written one over the other until nothing is discernible. Each item is scribbled randomly across the board, filling each space in a jumbled, tangled, multi-color mess. The white board represents my mind, my chatty, demanding, often jumbled thoughts.

As I sit down to meditate, I mentally reach for a dry erase marker and begin to erase the tangled mess, cleaning the board. Lovingly but thoroughly, each space on the white board is cleared until it is in fact pristine, clean, and once again white. Sometimes it takes me several minutes, breathing slowly and methodically erasing, clearing away and even scrubbing a bit. When the white board is clean, my mind becomes quiet.

Step Two – Listen.

In the quiet, allow space for what you hear or feel. Without judgement, observe your thoughts and feelings. Many things that pop up in meditation are familiar, a recording on a continuous loop, barking and wiggling for attention, like an eager inner terrier. Pat the terrier on the head and firmly say, "Kennel up, puppy. I can't play with you now." You may need to make this request several times before the terrier stays put in the kennel but be firm and insistent. *You* are in charge.

With a clean white board and the terrier in the kennel, we can be still and listen. Sometimes I simply listen to the quiet. Other times, I hear the deep, resonant truth of my highest self. Listen to your dreams and to every 'wouldn't-it-be-great-if' idea.

Step Three – Allow It To Unfold.

Balance the calendar and a rigid timeline with life's natural timing, rhythm, and flow. No need to hammer away, just show up each day, do the work, and let things unfold. While lists and timelines are wonderful tools, make space for the non-linear and the unexpected. By easing up a bit while still moving forward, we remove limits on the flow of creativity, dancing with the Universe as we co-create the outcome.

Step Four – Ask For Help.

Make peace with what you do not know and learn what you can. No need to bluff or pretend. Acknowledge what you do not know and actively seek support from others who do. I am amazed by how willing others are to teach me and guide me to resources simply because I asked. Remember always, the universe is friendly to our dreams. The needed stuff to make them real is often released in the simple act of asking.

Step Five – Act.

Take a small bit of productive, meaningful action each day toward the making of your life. When it all feels big and unwieldy, break it down to one simple step but please *do something,* no matter how small. This is where the list rightly resides. Let your inner organizer loose here and your efforts will gladly oblige. Place one bite-sized task on today's list and it just might happen taking you one step further.

Gather one new bit of information. Make one phone call. Eventually all those steps add up and your dreams will be closer.

This is what I call Life Making – The Art of Authentic Living. Worry not, you need not paint a masterpiece or write a book or build a tall building. Instead, set out to make your own, beautiful, meaningful, and authentic life. Bring your ideas and your true self forth today expressing YOU and offering you to the world. In doing so, you will feed, love, and nourish your soul. If this process does nothing more than help you to be more open-hearted, a little more creative and less fearful in the world, *it is enough*. In fact, this may be precisely what the world needs today.

When we clear a space, listen, allow, ask, and act, our daily actions and attention are put to work bringing forth our creative gifts and our very life. This is not small work. Nor is it unimportant. Our very well-being depends on the life we make. As does the well-being of the world.

My hope for you is that you gently bring yourself forth in both big and small ways, courageously expressing who you are, and nourishing the world. To do so is to come alive.

Spirit

Elizabeth Cabalka

Mystery

The most beautiful experience we can have is the mysterious. It is the fundamental emotion that stands at the cradle of true art and true science. – *Albert Einstein, The World As I See It*

There is so little room for mystery in our busy, fast paced, technologically-saturated world. With mobile devices affixed to our bodies and Google at-the-ready, there is nothing we cannot know.

I think that may not necessarily be a good thing. Personally, I enjoy pondering the unknown and inviting a bit of mystery into each day. In fact, I wonder if we lose something important in our rush to know. Is there a muscle that becomes underdeveloped when we do not wonder enough? Are we shutting the door on new ideas or an innovative solution by rushing to the internet for a factoid to fill the void, adopting someone else's answers for our pressing questions?

What if, just for a day or two, we pondered a bit more? What if we paused when faced with a question and, rather than jumping to fill the void, we left a space for something interesting? Perhaps what becomes most interesting in that space is an awareness of how anxious not-knowing makes us feel, begging the question, is it okay to not know?

Certainly there are pressing things each day for which it is critical to find an answer. Pronto! But not everything that sends us scurrying to the internet requires an answer right now.

Let's make space for mystery and pondering today, shall we? Let's wonder together and see what happens.

Inhale. Exhale. Repeat.

I need a breath of fresh air.

You take my breath away.

It is breathtaking.

I am out of breath.

I need to take a breather.

Give me room to breathe.

He was breathing down my neck.

Don't breathe a word.

Our breath is the most natural process in the body. Just look to our everyday language for our awareness of the importance of the breath. From the moment we let 'er rip in that first bawling breath to the moment of our last exhale, we are being breathed every moment of our existence. I say 'being breathed' because, for most of us, this simply happens. Thank goodness we do not have to think about the breath! It just happens. Inhale. Exhale. Repeat.

For millennia, the breath was thought to be inextricable from our being, our vitality and health, our awareness and our very essence. In *The Breathing Book*, author Donna Farhi shares the many languages that place breath front and center in the very nature of life. Here are a few in a long list:

· Greek: Psyche pneuma – breathe/soul/air/spirit
· Japanese: Ki – air/spirit
· Sanskrit: Prana – life force.

"The breath was seen as a force that ran through mind, body, and spirit like a river running through a dry valley giving sustenance to everything in its course," writes Farhi. "It is only in recent times have we reduced breathing to a mere respiratory exchange of carbon dioxide and oxygen."

While breath is with us throughout each moment of our existence, it has been uncommon in recent times to turn to our breath as a means of energizing, calming, or improving our well-being. I find this fascinating! Take a quick inventory of the refrigerator, pantry, medicine cabinet or liquor cabinet. That inventory will likely reveal several tools used to medicate for energy, self-soothing or relaxation. These are items that required money, time and energy to secure, shopping away as we breathed in and out, unaware of the magical medicine available in each breath.

Fortunately, people are waking up to the power of the breath. One self-proclaimed skeptical engineer in my Meditation and Mindfulness class marveled that the tools for relaxation he had been seeking for decades really were as close as his breath.

Inhale. Exhale. Repeat.

When faced with disease, weariness, anxiousness or fear, it is all too common to turn first to costly, external solutions that, in reality, only address symptoms but never touch the root of the problem. We turn to stimulants such as caffeine and nicotine for some pep, or to drugs, pills, and alcohol to chill out. As a society, we go to great lengths to artificially manipulate the body and mind, when some rudimentary skills and an awareness of the breath can naturally bring us clarity or even solutions for the challenges that cause us to reach for (*fill in the blank*).

Do not get me wrong. I love my coffee in the morning and I have done more anxiety eating in my life-time than I care to admit. Until several years ago, I was also part of the alarming statistic about women and wine. But lately, with a regular breath practice interwoven into my yoga practice, the cravings have subsided and a natural, light, grounded sense of being has kept me from scouring the cupboards, from seeking something exernal to change my feelings, to make me feel, or to not feel anything at all. Instead, a calm, deeply satisfied sense rests well in my bones. I still have my full catalog of life's problems. Breathing my way to clarity, however, keeps my head on straight and broadens my awareness of the banquet table of possible options.

I could go on at length about the toll of breathing badly but frankly that is boring. Instead, I would like to suggest that we consider the ease and fullness with which a child breathes. With that breath comes an aliveness and an unbridled joy. Spend ten minutes at a busy playground if you need a refresher on this simple life lesson. Hold the image of the joyful breath of a child as you move through the coming days. Throw your shoulders back, open your chest, and draw your next breath in, deep into the lungs filling them completely. As you exhale, draw the belly-button back toward the spine, wringing out all of the spent air, grateful that it served you well and making room for the next breath. Move gracefully and gratefully from the in-breath to the out-breath.

Inhale. Exhale. Repeat.

As you prepare for each day, breathe into and through your preparation. Visualize each breath infusing joy into each task. As you travel near and far, remain focused on the road and breathe deeply in the present, attuned and attentive especially when so many around you are likely not. When you gather with friends, breathe in and out your gratitude for those who share your days. Wait not to express your appreciation for their presence in your life, using your breath and voice. Breathe in and out, sending your breath into the world.

And, finally, with all this mindful breathing, notice a sense of well-being and joy spread outward from your heart. You created this sense of well-being. Just you and your breath. Inhale. Exhale. Repeat.

Elizabeth Cabalka

The Veil

Several years ago I was asked to speak at a church for All Saints day. The service was to be a celebration and a time for remembrance. As the author of a book about caring for my first husband, Charles, during his journey with terminal cancer, a friend felt I might have some words of wisdom to contribute to the service. While I felt flattered, frankly, I was stumped.

Charles was diagnosed with esophageal cancer in 1998 at the ripe old age of 39. He subsequently lived an amazing and inspiring three and one-half years after this diagnosis, passing away on Thanksgiving Day 2001. Since that day, I have heard his voice and felt his presence in numerous ways, including a drop of rain and box of greetings cards.

Contemplating the message for All Saints day, I sat at my computer searching aimlessly for the words that would somehow provide comfort to grieving individuals when I was knee-deep in my own grief and pain. My personal perplexity was wrapped in this ever-present irony: while I could no longer see or touch Charles, I believe he is always with me, part of me, around me, and very present. To be sure, during times of grief and loneliness, these thoughts were challenging to reconcile. Even so, my belief in his presence had been reinforced in many ways.

For example, I arrived home the day after his funeral, alone for the first time in days, to an empty house. It was a rainy, cold, gray November day, typical for Minnesota. As I reached up to close the garage door, dreading my trip down the walkway to a silent house, a drop of cool rain caressed my cheek. Wiping it away, I heard Charles's voice gently and clearly say, "I am the rain that touches your cheek. You are not alone." In that moment I found the strength to go inside the house and begin my life again.

Charles showed up again during an event he would have surely loved, the annual all-city garage sale in my quaint rural community, population 3,300. A few months earlier I purchased a home within the city limits and was able to host a garage sale with many of my new neighbors for the very first time. I sorted and tossed, priced, and boxed, then sorted some more until the day of the sale arrived. Anxious customers showed up at the door at dawn with dollars in hand and the big day began with a flurry of driveway commerce.

Charles always loved a good deal and a garage sale had good deal written all over it. He was a master at clipping coupons and the king of the mail-in rebate. Years earlier, one particularly good store coupon from the newspaper matched with an equally beneficial manufacturer's coupon reduced a much-loved breakfast cereal to mere pennies per box. For one week, the length of the promotion, Charles scoured recycling bins for coupons and made thrice daily trips to the grocery store using different check-out lanes each time. Seven days later we had our own personal stockpile of our favorite breakfast cereal. Fifty-two boxes to be exact. Yes, to say Charles loved a good deal was an enormous understatement.

As the garage sale began, I placed a box filled with a few hundred greetings cards on a TV tray outside the garage. Early in his career, Charles worked for a greeting card company and his remaining legacy was this stash of well wishes sorted neatly in a cardboard box, ten cents each and fifteen for one dollar. After the initial early morning rush of garage sale customers, there was a brief lull that sent me wandering among my possessions. My feet led me to the box of cards and I began to read and chuckle. Midway through the stack, I came across a piece of cardboard, a section divider, labeled in Charles's precise handwriting. *Miss You* was all it said. I clutched this message tightly to my chest and felt that Charles was with me. Such a priceless message there amidst the mundane.

Though eighteen months had passed since his death, it was as though he was standing right there beside me, overseeing it all wearing his unmistakable good deal grin. His presence felt so very real, but I told no one of my feelings and questioned my thoughts. "Was this real?" and "What is real anyway?" were questions I pondered as I made change for a dollar and bagged an old pair of ice skates.

A few minutes later, I wandered back to the box of greeting cards, feeling both hesitant and more than a little confused. Toward the back of the box, a second cardboard divider provided an answer to my inner questioning. Once again labeled in Charles's precise handwriting, the transcendent message simply read *I Love You.* Nothing more.

That Saturday morning, standing in my driveway I fully understood that the veil is so thin between what we see and what we cannot see. We are inextricably connected by the love we share. This was Charles's message to me in the unexpected raindrop and a box of old greeting cards on a TV tray in the driveway.

Eighty-Eight Hawks

I have had so many incredible teachers in my life. I am a product of public education and a mighty proud product at that. My music teachers were not only teachers but also became dear friends as I reached adulthood. My English teachers pushed and prodded the love of great literature into my being year after year, as well as the basics of the five paragraph essay. (A powerful combination that helped form my current vocation.) When people ask if I have always been a writer, I often credit my English teachers with planting the seeds of this creative endeavor.

The earth and all its creatures are also my teachers. The great wave of growth in the spring makes me positively giddy, the cycles of the moon influence my energy and some bodily functions, and I cheer on the trees as they perform their color-filled hoorah each autumn. I closely follow the migration of the birds and modify my daily activities with the ebb and flow of daylight.

I grew up on a lake and spent much of my life in or on it, depending on the season. The majority of my childhood activities involved water in its various forms, frozen or liquid. My childhood chores involved bailing the boats and sweeping goose poop off the dock. Grass, water, trees, and weather were key factors in my youth and continue to exercise great influence over me today. I am most discontented when I am amidst miles of concrete, neon lights, and artificial noise. My soul sings as I walk along the lake in the early morning, the sun rising and the tall grasses awaiting a dance with the wind.

This was one reason I was initially drawn to Charles. In him I found great kinship in my love of the world around me. The first day we met, we were tapping maple trees to make maple syrup and I quietly rejoiced as he whispered both an apology and thanks to the huge tree before he pounded the spigot into its bark and hung the bucket. One week before his cancer diagnosis in the spring of 1998, we took a memorable walk in the woods where he stopped to wrap his arms around his favorite tree and press his face against the trunk. On many a summer morn he stepped out onto the walkway in front of our isolated wooded home, clad in his briefs and a t-shirt, throwing open his arms in an embrace of the new day. In Charles I saw reflected my own unapologetic childlike appreciation of nature.

The hawk has long been my spirit guide, an outward sign that affirms me with a gentle nudge *yes*. I do not know how or when I came to know this. Growing up in a fairly traditional Methodist family, such monikers as 'spirit guide' were not a part of my daily vocabulary or consciousness, yet my guides were very real. In my twenties, I became aware of the hawk's presence especially in times of confusion. As I pondered a particularly pesky life-event, I would invariably look up, only to see the underside of a hawk soaring overhead, hearing the gentle 'yes' in my heart, affirming what I knew. Some might call this coincidence while other call it a sign or a visible answer to prayer. Whatever the label, the hawk was particularly comforting as I grieved the death of Charles, losing him to cancer when I was thirty-seven years old. When everything seemed unknown or unclear, there were periodic moments of clarity.

A particularly poignant insight was provided by two hawks a few months before Charles died. It was a gorgeous unseasonably warm Sunday morning, the sunshine warming my car as I drove east on a rolling country road near our home. My sun roof was open and provided a functional frame for a stunning nature tableau above the road. As I watched, two hawks soared effortlessly in a perfectly round invisible loop, the line between them expertly bisecting the circle of their flight. I stopped the car beneath them, not quite one mile from our driveway, opened my door and stepped out, leaning against the car and craning my neck upward. I quietly cheered them on as the danced together, red and gold against the blue sky. I could imagine the deeply resonant sound their circling would make if it took place on the rim of a crystal glass. This was perfection.

After a full minute, the circular dance began to take on a different form, each creature tracing its own circle with its wings. Then one circle became two, as they slowly stirred the sky above my car. Their velocity never changed, yet their circles were now connected only in one spot, like the intersection of two parts of a snowman. Their ballet with the currents, once so perfectly choreographed together, was now taking them in their own separate directions.

I silently watched my own life play out in the sky above me. After another minute, the two circles began to move further apart, connecting less and less frequently until they were completed separate, one to my north and one to my south. I could not take my eyes off this display, beautiful and terrible, natural and deeply personal. I stood leaning against my car, weeping as the two hawks parted company and continued their dance apart. As the tears wet my cheeks, I was surprised to hear my voice yell, "No!" at the sky and at God.

Prior to this event I teetered daily on the ledge between joy and despair, denial and acceptance, as I watched Charles's body fail. Until this road-side event, there had been room in my heart for the glimmer of possibility that this was some sort mistake and Charles would live. As I wearily climbed back in the driver's seat and started the car, I was aware that I could no longer pretend that Charles would live beyond the coming months. Our dance was already taking us in different directions, the circles of our lives connecting less and less frequently as he spent most of his days barely present, circling the door to the unknown.

This awareness of our increasingly separate ballet battered my soul, not harshly but like a persistent wave erodes the shore. My grieving took on a new form that day, now unavoidable and inescapable.

After Charles died, the world around me continued to affirm and guide me in my new life alone. After living in our home for eleven months after his death, I sold or gave away nearly half of everything I owned, moved the rest into storage, and packed my computer and some clothing in my car. A friend in New Mexico opened her home to me for a few months and I was leaving all I knew, family and friends, routine and well-worn paths, for a grand adventure.

My friend, Rob, flew in to join me in the long drive, the journey into my new life. As I took one last walk through the now-empty house I felt conflicted. Was I abandoning Charles in some way by leaving this place, a thought especially heinous because of my tingling excitement? As I looked around me, I noted that the walls were empty and there was nothing to cling to, my anchor to this place was gone. It was time to move on.

I closed the front door one last time, climbed into the car and drove away, looking back only once. By the time we reached the end of the driveway and made our way to the county road, I was nearly giddy with the thrill of all that was unknowable and awaiting my arrival, at the same time asking myself, "Am I doing the right thing?"

My answer appeared almost immediately, perched on a roadside post. A plump, golden hawk ruffled its feathers as we passed, then took flight in my rear view mirror, soaring over the road.

"Yes," I said aloud, smiling at my questioning companion in the passenger seat. "Yes."

With that, we drove toward my new life on County Road #3, turning right at the intersection of possibility and the unknown.

As we drove the roads that led south and west, I was often affirmed by my spirit guides. In the 1,485 miles from my door to my new adventure, I saw not just one but eight-eight hawks. Each one providing a ripple of excitement and certainty as the scenery changed along the road. They weren't the answer, simply the resounding affirmation to everything I already knew.

I am grateful for this overwhelming outward show of clarity because I saw no hawks during my five months away. But the constant nudging on that long drive imprinted a mark of certainty on my southwest days. That mark on my consciousness was like a thin white fading scar I could touch when in doubt and remember how it came to be. As I grieved Charles in this new location, it was with a certainty that I was where I needed to be and all was well.

So much has transpired since that sunny November day when I began the trek to New Mexico. On the outside, my life is unrecognizable. What remains the same is my desire to discern my direction then follow the path that is before me without hesitation. Fortunately, the world around me still provides answers in nearly every moment, sometimes a soft whispered 'Yes' of a falling leaf, often a precise 'Yes!' of a soaring hawk.

I seek clarity daily for answers to my frequent questions. How shall I spend my day? Whom shall I help? What am I to learn? How can I be of the greatest service? To my delight, my questions are often answered in my own back yard.

Seeds

An infinity of forests lie dormant in the dreams of an acorn. – *Dr. Wayne Dyer*

I recently awoke to a great bit of clarity.

For the last eight years, I have held fast to a dream – a vision for my future. I have never wavered in my desire but it has never been clear how and when this dream would come together.

I recently realized that the answer I have been so impatiently and laboriously seeking – the key to unlock that realization of that dream – is simply not yet ready to manifest. It is not yet fully formed. To be sure, it is coming, being shaped now in that cosmic goo of all-possibility. My job is to be patient, to work daily toward it, to wait, to calmly

remain certain of its arrival, and to trust I will recognize it when it shows up.

Several years ago, one of my mentors taught me about Law of Gestation, one of the many universal laws, like the Law of Gravity. He described the Law of Gestation in this way: Everything begins as a seed. Some are physical seeds, like a carrot seed, an apple seed or a baby seed. Some seeds are non-physical, like the seed of an idea.

All these seeds have their own gestation period, their own time in which they are formed. Asking for an idea to manifest before its time is like the father-to-be asking his four-month pregnant wife, "So, where's the baby already?!"

The problem is that most people do not know how to plant one idea, tend it lovingly, hold the vision of what it can become, while also allowing it to be formed in partnership with the wildly creative universe.

Most people just plant and plant and plant. Then, impatient and disillusioned, they walk away from the field prematurely seeking a new field in which to plant more seeds.

One day they loudly and resolutely proclaim, 'Oak Tree!' The next day, they shout 'Turnip!' or 'Apple Tree!'. What they do not know is that the moment they proclaim, 'Oak Tree!' the acorn-looking seed of an idea is planted in the rich soil of possibility. If the conditions are right, so much starts to happen immediately, just below the surface. By the time the first itty-bitty shoot breaks through the soil, the pulse of that beautiful idea – 'Oak Tree!' – is drawing to it all manner of matter to make it so. Most simply do not tend the seed and wait for the harvest.

At the same time, some people spend all their waking energy tending the seeds of precisely what they do *not* want. All focus and energy is directed to the worst case scenario, toward what they fear most or what they hate. This also plants seeds that are all too often rigorously tended. Sadly, these are the folks that are consistently and wildly (yet unknowingly) successful, living daily with their abundant harvest.

In my meditation this evening I was reminded of the holiness of waiting for the beautiful all-possibleness. The holiness of trusting. The holiness of actually delighting in anticipation of the arrival of the fully matured seed that is forming at this very moment. There is growth in that seed and growth within us too as we work and wait, tend and nurture.

Oh, and that dream that I have tended for eight long years? It showed up fully formed and the pathway is now clear. All is ready. It arrived right on time, more magnificent that I could have ever imagined.

The Unexpected

I am a fan of the unexpected. To be sure, this was not always the case. I was once ruled by my Franklin Planner, color coded, labeled, neatly printed, with an accounting for each hour of the day. The unexpected fit precisely nowhere into my leather bound three-ring binder. The unexpected was in fact my enemy. While I still have an impressively rigorous schedule these days, I have come to love the unexpected.

Honestly, I am not entirely sure how or when this change occurred. Maybe it is my advancing age and the recognition that I am not in charge of everything and everyone. Or maybe it is a deepening awareness that life's great richness often comes unbidden, utterly disregarding my carefully made plans.

These days, I often see the unexpected as an opportunity to slow down or to see something differently. If I happen to be following someone who is driving slowly, I guess I was meant to slow down and exercise a little patience. I will get there eventually. If someone is gruff or unkind, they may be suffering and perhaps it is an opportunity to wish them well. How we see the unexpected and how we respond is always a choice.

One spring day I passed one of my favorite trees in the 21,000 acre mountain regional park we called home for many winters. A large portion of the park was claimed by a wildfire in 1995 and visible remnants remain of this powerful event. I often passed one seemingly dead tree and never cease to marvel at its elegance, its lines so shapely yet sparse against a mountainous background.

Every spring the most interesting and unexpected thing happens to this dead tree. A Brittle Bush plant, normally a ground dweller, blooms smack dab in the gathering point of several branches a full four feet off the ground. Prolific yellow blossoms decorate this otherwise sparse tableau.

Another amazing thing happens in the desert each spring time. Glorious blossoms turn up in unlikely places. My personal favorite is a desert underdog called the Buck Thorn cholla. For much of the year, it appears prickly and barren. In the springtime, however, Suessical-looking reddish-purple spikes appear around several tight buds at the end of each spindly limb.

While the thorns of this cactus are as sharp as expected, new spikey growths surrounding the bud are rubbery feeling and fun to touch. The bud grows rapidly making daily walks in the desert a thrill.

The Buck Thorn cholla taught me much during my twelve winters in the desert. When I first arrived, I gravitated to the showy blossoms of the prickly pear cactus, Mexican poppies and purple lupine. My Minnesota-trained eyes initially latching firmly upon the brilliant colors.

Only after fully acquainting myself with the Buck Thorn and receiving abundant rewards for my patience and attention, did I fully realize its beauty wrapped in the unexpected. Not just the beauty of the glorious but short lived blossom but also the beauty of its becoming! The beauty of anticipating what will soon be revealed. The beauty of appreciating the promise that lies deep within that unexpected, unruly, spindly, sharp, and deceptively dull plant.

The Buck Thorn cholla taught me to look closely at those things I am tempted to ignore or treat as unremarkable or even see as ugly. I learned to find the mystery they hold inside them and trust there is much happening that I cannot see.

As I look back on the difficulties in my life, I now see them quite differently, more like I now see the Buck Thorn cholla. When it all hits that fan and feels ugly or prickly, I often take a breath and remind myself that beauty is coming in unexpected ways. Even if the only beauty is the fact that this ugliness will make me stronger and wiser, that the gifts of wisdom I receive for slogging on through are mine forever.

What if we all looked at the difficult circumstances as unexpected life-lessons and beheld the prickly people around us with new eyes? What could they teach us? What beauty lies within? What gifts patiently await our curiosity and attention?

Authentic Living

Coming Home

There's no place like home.
There's no place like home.
There's no place like home.

- Dorothy Gale, The Wizard of Oz

After 47,250 miles, I have made my way home.

Several years ago as a young widow, I met a man and fell in love. Both rebuilding our lives, we together experienced a cosmic do-over and created a new life together. For many years, we divided our time between Minnesota and Arizona. We made two beautiful lives, each textured and full and rich but so distinct. We marked the passage of time not by the calendar but by events and friends here and by events and friends there, as well as our seasonal cross-country commute.

It all began with a five state book tour in the spring of 2004 after my first book, *Wednesdays at the Fluff 'n' Fold*, was published. We subsequently traversed the country twenty-four times, a Powell and Hyde spinning cable car of sorts, albeit more fluid in the route but just as 'A to B and back' with equally purposeful pirouettes on each end.

Our migratory pathway provided a windshield view of the evolution of ten states. We watched towns grow and whither, noting the impact of the economy and the elements on the landscape. We traveled in white knuckle conditions and shared achingly beautiful vistas. The miles in between our two lives held both long conversations and companionable silence, hours of seventy miles per hour stillness.

I loved the commute, especially the psychological commute. Traversing the miles, watching the landscape change with the passing of days, this was my bi-annual reset. As the landscape, colors, and architecture changed, so did my inner rhythm, recalculating an inner sense of home. A twice yearly 1,765 mile moving meditation.

In our many years of travel, I experienced home in three distinct ways:

A place I point to on a map and claim as part of me. The acreage that holds deep memories and some of my formative becoming, for better or for worse. At home here I am a thread woven into the fabric of a place and it in me. The place of my people. This is one experience of home.

A sense of home that traveled with me, transplanted in another location. While not the place of my birth, it is where I made a life, delivered there on a fortuitous wind of change. A hearty perennial that took root, first sleeping, then creeping and finally leaping in the way of perennials. Strangers became family and an adopted place also became home.

And finally, I experience home not as a place at all, **but as a returning to myself,** found within a moment of mindfulness. Each inhale and each exhale leading me back from *what if?* or *what now?* grounding in this moment, fully rooted in my body. Present. Here. Now. Connected. In this I also experience home.

In life's coming and going, home can feel illusive, displaced by restlessness, conditions, hardship or longing. Whether knocked off course by circumstance, inconvenience or disaster, we can become lost, untethered from solid ground, and from our sense of place. Far from home and feeling disconnected. My pathway home is found in daily self-care.

Yoga Expression Spirit – my map, sextant and stars – recalculate my internal GPS, always leading me home. Pick one and see if you find yourself circling back home.

Yoga – Roll out your yoga mat, listen to your body, breathe fully and very gently stretch. Feel yourself settle back into your flesh and bones, no longer brittle, now supple and fluid.

Expression – Unleash your creativity! Find your palette in your garden, in a hummed or whistled tune, or perhaps in the kitchen. Play! Imagine art class and recess all in one.

Spirit – Sit quietly for a few moments, feeling the ocean of your breath wash in and then wash out, the tide touching your heart and then rolling outward. Spend a moment at home and at one with mystery.

Where has your journey taken you today? Have you gone walkabout perhaps or are you at home?

Where Do You Live?

The only true address for fully alive living is:
You – Mentally and Physically,
c/o Your Body
This Present Moment, Here and Now.

"Do you live around here?"

Most of us are fortunate to be able to respond to that question with a yes or a no. We can also provide directions to a spot on the map where our stuff is located. This location likely has universally recognized coordinates with which it is identified. Most call this space 'home', but is that really where we live?

In the Meditation and Mindfulness course I teach, nearly every participant acknowledges and laments the fact that they spend nearly all their time in their head, utterly captive to and tossed about by their persistent thoughts. Unable to stop or even calm their racing mind, they arrive in class exhausted and nearly desperate to stop the perpetual inner chatter.

For many of us, the mind chatters away, day and night, waking or sleeping, coloring every experience and robbing us of peace. Living exclusively in the mind, we also become disconnected from the body, ignoring its needs and signals, surrendered by default to a two-dimensional, less-than-resourceful life. Many simply experience this as a deep sense of unrest. The inevitable answer to "Where do you live?" is all too often "In my head."

At the same time, the question is not only "Where do you live?" but "*When* do you live?" If you are not living in the present moment, you are most likely leasing an empty space in a past that no longer exists, in a future that is yet to be formed or perhaps in a space that belongs to someone else – a refugee of sorts, cast out by your own mental devices.

So, where do you live? When do you live? These questions call for a bit of reflection as the answers – your mailing address and your experiential address – have natural outcomes. They shape your experience of life as well as your biology.

As I mentioned previously, my husband and I enjoyed a life lived in two states for twelve years. We forged beautiful friendships, adopted much-loved past-times, joined meaningful organizations and, yes, we enjoyed the warmth of each Arizona winter. Our snow bird life of a dozen years and the people we met shaped who we are, providing life-changing, course-altering gifts too numerous to thoroughly catalog.

And then, one day, it was time once again to redefine our understanding of home, no longer dividing our lives.

The many friendships we shaped over the years now travel with us in our hearts as we return to our roots and to family in Minnesota. There is no more running. It is time to be here now and it is good.

Surprising Gifts

As I initially exhaled into this change, I noticed a deep and wide sense of spaciousness as I considered both the calendar and the clock. From 2005 to 2016, we moved twice per year – twenty four moves. Think about that for a moment. Only now I am recognizing how this ping-pong life both blessed me greatly and fragmented my inner being.

For over a decade, we were nearly always preparing to leave, in transit or settling in, reacquainting and regaining our feet, and figuring out once again where the doggone can opener is located. Around the edges of each transition, we were either leaning forward and planning or looking back and pining, and fully present only for a small window of time. In addition, a perpetual sense of urgency helped populate the calendar, accompanied with an underlying sense of *not enough time*.

Our first autumn in a long time without a seasonal migration, brought a deep sense of spaciousness and great anticipation. There was no packing and mending, no tossing and preparing. Instead, there was the opportunity to be present to the change of seasons, within my being and in the world around me. I took time to be still and witness the autumnal splendor, without boundary, deadline, or interruption.

The dahlias in my garden had their full expression, even touching snow. Previously they were unceremoniously yanked from the ground in their peak of bloom, the crimson buds and blossoms cut off and the bulbs tossed in a bucket to winter beneath the basement stairs. As we pulled away from our home each autumn, in the peak of the fall colors, I often felt a bit like those red dahlias. Plucked from the ground too soon without full expression.

Resettling in our century-old cottage also brought a welcome sense of rootedness and firm footing on solid ground. I am no longer hedging my bets emotionally and steeling myself for the sure to come heartache twice yearly departures bring. In this rootedness I am finding a welcome sense of spaciousness and possibility, both touched by a hint of sadness from missing true and dear friends and winter warmth.

At a deeper level, I believe we are meant to be here in this place for reasons not yet revealed. Perhaps it is time to create something fully, not simply planting and running, planting and running. This change of address – mentally and physically – will no doubt shape us too in ways unforeseen. I chose to see it as a gift and look forward to unwrapping it.

It is with this same sensibility that I come often to my yoga mat, to ground myself in my body and in a sense of place, planted firmly here with deep roots.

With each breath and each posture, I call myself home.

What about you? What is your address? Where and when do you live? How does this shape you? Is anyone home?

What Brings You Alive?

Anything or anyone that does not bring you alive is too small for you. – *David Whyte, excerpt from the poem Sweet Darkness.*

"What brings you alive?" a friend inquired recently. What a wonderful question! We were reconnecting over coffee after many years apart and she shared the story of how she came alive to her life.

Several years ago she realized that the walls of her life were pressing inward. Her world had somehow become smaller when she was not looking. Her daily thoughts were often repeats or left-overs from yesterday's thoughts. Her routines and actions were familiar enough that she needed to give them little or no thought. As a result, she spent much of each day on autopilot, her mental activity taking her far from her body. Her relationship was flat and she didn't even care enough to muster the energy to break it off. She did her work and collected her pay. Each day looked just like yesterday and tomorrow would almost certainly look like today. Her inner and outer worlds had both become small. She was bored and numb, no longer actively seeking the interesting or the engaging.

Listening to the radio one day as she drove home from work, a phrase from David Whyte's poem Sweet Darkness jolted her out of her autopilot afternoon and caused her to sit up.

"What brings me alive?" she wondered aloud.

Her immediate response was, "Not a doggone thing. I feel dead."

With eyes suddenly brimming and a knot in her throat, she turned into a parking lot to collect herself. "Oh, honestly, when did I become so *small?*" she wailed.

This event took place two weeks before her fiftieth birthday and shifted the plate tectonics of her inner world. In addition, a colleague died suddenly a few days prior bringing mortality to the forefront of her newly awakened thoughts, sprinkling more than a dash of urgency on her parking lot moment.

"Enough!" she proclaimed. "I need more! I want to LIVE!"

Ten years later, she sat before me gloriously, beautifully, vibrantly alive. With persistence and grace, she transformed her world into one that beautifully supports the expansive possibilities of her life. As I listened I was fascinated. What did she do? How did she start? What insights could she share?

I learned that my friend made no grand gestures ten years ago, other than to commit to coming alive in some way each day. In both big and small ways, she chose to wake up, choosing activities, people and thoughts that bring her alive.

Her pathway of awakening was that of a student. For the past ten years, my friend has taken one class at a time, year round, many of which were free or inexpensive. You name it, she has likely studied it. She has taken classes through local Community Ed and the YMCA, a nearby community college, through the public library, with the county's artist guild, on a local farm, at her church and even in a few in exotic places.

This single action of becoming a dedicated student opened her thinking to new and interesting ideas. She met other students with shared interests, she read books she would not have otherwise read. She thought thoughts and had experiences that were new and compelling. She wrote papers, created artwork, created a hay bale garden, learned to speak Spanish, learned to swim, made pottery, studied history, joined Toast Masters, rode the light rail, wrote poetry, took piano lessons, took a statistics class (really!), volunteered at a women's shelter, and became legally ordained to act as the marriage officiant for two dear friends.

What I find equally compelling is the fact that she lives in the same house, has the same job, the same boyfriend (now husband) and even the same dog as she did ten years ago. As she likes to say, she changed her mind but not her address and changed her entire world.

The new skills she learned and interests she developed caused her to see her world differently. Her curiosity for people and ideas spurred her into conversations that were enriching and into unforeseen friendships. She did not get a Ph.D., sky dive or dance naked in public. No, nothing drastic. She simply engaged daily in the world around her and it brought her alive.

What brings you alive? What quickens your pulse in anticipation? Conversely, what brings blessed stillness to your inner workings? Is there something that is inviting you to see, think, do or be more? Are there mundane things you can release to make room for something that really interests you? If your life feels small, please push a little at the boundaries of your world. That is the only way to stop it from growing even smaller. Start today. Start right now. One step. Begin.

Your actions need not be earth shattering but please do *something* that brings you out of yourself, that causes you to look up and look around. Perhaps take a different route home from work. Buy one new food item at the grocery store. Have a conversation with someone you do not know or perhaps looks a little different. Read a book by a new author. Volunteer. Become curious and ask questions of complete strangers. Consider another viewpoint. Hand write a letter. Try something that scares you just a little bit. Talk to your neighbor.

How about a random act of kindness? As you look back at the end of the day, has something opened up? Is it brighter inside? Do you feel more alive?

Today is the day, a birthday of sorts. Wake up. Look up. Engage in your authentic life. You can do this. Choose something that brings you alive.

Revere the Rake?

The shovel is a prayer to the farmer's foot as he steps down and the soft earth gives way.
– Carrie Newcomer

Yoga **E**xpression **S**pirit are effective and powerful tools with which I have reshaped my life. I love these tools and they serve me well. I have also been fortunate to work with others using these tools, witnessing their transformation, large and small. By their very nature, tools allow us to create, to unearth, to move, and to shape. In the act of creating, where would we be without our tools?

Just as we have tools for the garden, however, we do not generally revere the rake and spade. Instead, we delight in the act of gardening and give thanks for the harvest. By all means, feel deeply grateful for the tools that help you craft your garden.

Certainly dabble with several tools, finding those that fit your hands, and even become proficient if you choose.

Do not lose sight, however, of the process of shaping and tending your garden, your hands in the soil, the movement of your body, the scent of growth, the incremental daily deepening of roots, the forming of buds and fruit. Marvel at the unique unfolding of each growing thing and notice how plants interact with each other, with sunlight, with moisture, and with you. Let the colors fill your vision. Feel delight in your co-creative role. It is here that your body, mind, breath, and efforts are united with mystery in the making of your garden. Your joy can be found here where your authentic life is made.

If you have set your sights on reclaiming your authentic life, **Y**oga **E**xpression **S**pirit are fine and effective tools. As you use them to shape and tend your life, may they also bring your life vibrancy, delight and joy, and help shape the person you wish to become. This is the harvest of your authentic life.

Say YES to Your Authentic Life

So, here we are, friend.

You have come this far. Your authentic life awaits. You now have the tools. The seeds are planted. Now is the time.

I invite you to climb out of that cramped space in your head. Return to your body and engage kindly in a measure of self-care, body, mind, and breath.

I invite you to give attention to your inner longings. Turn and face them fully. Give them your hands and your voice and your time. Bring them forth. Give them life. Delight as they take shape.

I invite you to make a place for mystery in your life, inviting the unknown to dance with you daily. Make a place at the table for the unexpected guest.

More than anything, I invite you to step into all of who you are. Stand tall and proud, owning your uniqueness.

I invite you to say YES to your authentic life.

Acknowledgements

I am so grateful to be surrounded by wise teachers, loving family, and treasured friends. The colorful threads of your wisdom, love, humor, friendship, grace, and guidance are all woven into everything I am and all I create. The texture of my work and my life is far more durable, resilient, and lovely because of you. I am so very grateful to each of you.

Those who were particularly instrumental in shaping this work have my unending gratitude. They are Deb Barr and Dona Schallenkamp, meditation buddies extraordinaire; Cyd Malouf, my playful, supremely kind, and always supportive friend; Jill Bishop, my sounding board, after countless miles and hours together, our walking conversation continues; Marcia Appel, wise teacher whose insights helped shape this book. And Michael, the captain of my cheering section. Every one of you is a precious gift to me.

Elizabeth Cabalka

Artwork

I have been fortunate to know John Gerber since the late seventies. I value his creativity and friendship in equal measure. His artwork has been invaluable in shaping the vision of **Y**oga **E**xpression **S**pirit.

Do yourself an enormous favor and acquaint yourself with his work. May you also be fortunate enough to someday meet this remarkable artist.

Website: www.johngerber.com

Follow John on Facebook at GerbertArt

About the Author

Elizabeth Cabalka is an author, meditation and yoga instructor, and blogger. Her great passion is supporting individuals in their journey of self-discovery.

Follow Elizabeth's Blog at

yogaexpressionspirit.wordpress.com

For information about her classes, retreats and workshops, or for press inquiries and speaking engagements, please email:

elizabethcabalkaauthor@gmail.com

Author photo by Amanda Dambowy